Navigating the Mortgage Maze

Navigating the Mortgage Maze

THE SIMPLE TRUTH ABOUT FINANCING YOUR HOME

Dale Vermillion

NORTHFIELD PUBLISHING

CHICAGO

All Scripture quotations, unless otherwise indicated, are taken from the *Holy Bible, New Living Translation*, copyright © 1996, 2004. Used by permission of Tyndale House Publishers, Inc., Wheaton, Illinois 60189, U.S.A. All rights reserved.

Scripture quotations marked NIV are taken from the *Holy Bible, New International Version*®. NIV®. Copyright © 1973, 1978, 1984 by International Bible Society. Used by permission of Zondervan. All rights reserved.

Editor: Jim Vincent
Cover design: John Hamilton Design
Interior design: Smartt Guys design

Library of Congress Cataloging-in-Publication Data

Vermillion, Dale.
  Navigating the mortgage maze : the simple truth about financing your home /
Dale Vermillion.
    p. cm.
  Includes bibliographical references.
  ISBN 978-0-8024-8311-9
  1. Mortgage loans—United States. 2. House buying—United States—Costs. I. Title.

HG2040.5.U5V47 2009
332.7'22—dc22

                          2008034447

The material presented in this book is not intended to replace professional counsel. Neither the publisher nor the author assumes responsibility for adverse consequences resulting from application of advice presented here.

We hope you enjoy this book from Northfield Publishing. Our goal is to provide high-quality, thought-provoking books and products that connect truth to your real needs and challenges. For more information on other books and products written and produced from a biblical perspective, go to www.moodypublishers.com or write to:

Northfield Publishing
215 West Locust Street
Chicago, IL 60610

1 3 5 7 9 10 8 6 4 2

Printed in the United States of America

CONTENTS

To my beautiful wife and best friend, Laurel,
the most unselfish, caring, kind and humble person I have ever known.
You have showed me what love and friendship really are.
Thank you for supporting me through many years of work and travel,
and for exemplifying how to truly love God and others.

ACKNOWLEDGMENTS

Many people helped me to navigate through the writing of the *Mortgage Maze* book. None have helped more than my family. I'm grateful to my wife, Laurel, for her input, wisdom, encouragement and prayers. My mom and dad, Dorothy and George, who have loved me always, also made such a book possible. You taught me right from wrong and the importance of integrity and hard work. My thanks as well to my four children: Brock, Jake, Beau, and Jessica, for so many laughs, so many fun times, so many great memories. I love and am so proud of each of you.

I also acknowledge my staff (and my buddies), Lynne Knutson and Anne McClane, for their input, guidance, and prayers in writing this book.

I'm grateful to Mark Berg and John Yukawa for their financial expertise, and to Steve Sager for his tax and accounting expertise. The many great mortgage professionals I have worked with and learned from over the years are also responsible for my refining the topics in *Navigating the Mortgage Maze*.

Moody Publishers has given me great support and advice in developing my first book. Special thanks to Steve Lyon for his patience, leadership, and belief in me, and to Jim Vincent for his great editing input.

I am grateful to Dan Hayes and the 24/7 youth group for their friendship and prayers, as well as those friends and members of VCG who prayed for me and this book (too many to name).

For their guidance over the years, thanks to pastors Glenn Horne, Zack Turner, Todd Habegger, and Jim Young.

Finally, I acknowledge Jesus Christ, my Savior, for rescuing me, blessing me with so much, for loving me unconditionally, and for making me a new man. I owe everything to Him.

GETTING THROUGH THE
Maze

Record Foreclosures Sweep America"; "Home Values Plunge"; "Deceptive Mortgage Practices Exposed"; "Another Financial Institution Fails." All those headlines appeared in 2007 and 2008 as homeowners endured what financial experts may one day call the worst mortgage and real estate debacle of all time.

What happened? There has been no shortage of opinions and views expressed to try and answer that question. Nearly everyone is looking to find the root cause to point the blame at something or someone. The simple truth is that the causes were so widespread and involved so many conditions, companies, and individuals that there is plenty of blame to go around. The more important question today is "What can you and I do now to improve whatever situation we are in and then make sure it does not happen again?" That is what this book is about.

This book is not about the hows of the recent collapse but about the "how tos":

- How to choose the right mortgage and mortgage provider so that you can survive future up-and-down housing markets

- How to be prepared in future transactions so you can protect yourself from repeat occurrences
- How to buy a home or refinance your mortgage and put yourself in the best possible position for true financial strength and independence
- How to understand the opportunities locked inside your home's equity and use them to achieve your financial goals
- How to approach mortgage financing as an investment, not a debt
- How to eliminate the debt that has so burdened us so we can take back control of our finances!

By being properly educated and knowing the truths about handling a mortgage, we can avoid many of the problems in the future. That's what this book offers: a way to navigate through the maze to buy the right home or refinance with the right kind of mortgage.

A book on mortgage financing may not seem as interesting as a John Grisham novel. But as you read through this book you will uncover fascinating aspects of mortgage financing and debt management. You will be introduced to revolutionary concepts and strategies for handling your mortgage. It's important reading. After all, your home mortgage is most likely the largest financial transaction you will ever make, and it is a central part of your overall financial well-being.

Think of it. A mortgage is a vital part of our overall financial health, stability, and success. Because our home's equity is usually the largest asset we own, a mortgage loan can be our greatest resource for the cash we need for major life events:

buying homes, critical life purposes, consolidating debts, paying major expenses, even planning for retirement. Therefore, we don't want to enter into one of the largest and most important financial decisions *uneducated, unprepared,* and *overwhelmed.*

Chasing Our Anxieties

The complexities and components of a mortgage loan and the technical nature of a mortgage transaction often bring homeowners anxiety and concern. An Associated Press–AOL survey in 2008 found that one in seven people worry that they can't make their mortgage payments.[1] Richard Chaifetz, CEO of ComPsych, a Chicago-based employee-assistance firm that offers employees wellness and crisis intervention services, recently reported that financial worries have "escalated to the No. 1 issue because of the housing crisis." Calls to ComPsych in 2008 about financial worries surged 20 percent over the previous year; those related to mortgage problems doubled.[2] This book was written to address those concerns and simplify the complexities into an easy-to-understand guide to getting the best loan for your situation, qualifications, and future.

Although the mortgage industry is an ever-changing and cyclical industry, the tools and techniques you will learn in this book are timeless. The fact is, although the mortgage and financial sectors are constantly in flux, the desire for homeownership is constant; it is the American Dream! The need to use equity to access money is not going away and has always been the most beneficial way for homeowners to access cash. Simultaneously, the desire to get out of debt is one that we all dream about—one that I will help you master. What you learn in this book can help you not just for today, but for the rest of your life.

Navigating will tackle nearly every aspect of mortgage financing—from acquiring a new mortgage loan to managing the one you have today. It will help you understand interest rates, mortgage transactions, debt, and personal finances. At times I will deal with some very analytical concepts, but I will break them down into bite-size pieces so you can understand them and walk away with facts to support the strategies you will learn. I will give you examples, stories, facts, and timeless truths that you will be able to easily relate to, and practical strategies you can easily adapt and implement going forward to have power over your financial future. This book will help you to develop a strategy for your current and future mortgage decisions that will save you thousands, maybe even tens or hundreds of thousands, of dollars!

The Unknown Possibilities of Mortgage Financing

Imagine that you could achieve some or all of the following on your next mortgage *refinance*:

- Negotiate an excellent interest rate with very competitive fees.
- Have the optimum monthly payments for your situation.
- Save thousands of dollars both in the short and long term.
- Free up thousands in cash from your equity with potentially little or no impact on your payment.
- Reduce your income taxes.
- Eliminate your debt and mortgage balance faster.
- Own your home free and clear sooner.

- Save tens (if not hundreds) of thousands of dollars in interest.
- Save thousands up front in monthly payments.

Imagine many of those outcomes at no net cost to you!

This may seem hard to believe, but many of these things are possible through prudent mortgage financing. In fact, this is exactly the kind of beneficial mortgage loan that your loan officer should have told you about. It is the kind you will be able to negotiate on your own from now on!

The Truth Revealed

Millions of consumers, like you, borrow against their home every year. The majority of borrowers entrust a mortgage professional who is, for all intents and purposes, a complete stranger to guide them through a mortgage transaction. This is a process that none of us like, and that frequently results in a loan we ultimately cannot live with! Throughout this book you will be educated in every aspect of mortgage financing so you can navigate the mortgage transaction: understanding and negotiating rates and fees; the benefits of homeownership; utilizing your equity for debt elimination and cash; lowering your payments; and reducing your taxes. In addition, by the end of this book you'll be able to navigate the mortgage process.

A Mortgage Is Money

How do you define a mortgage? I am certain that most of you would struggle with this question and the answer will almost always be complex and confusing. Most likely, somewhere in your definition words like *rate, transaction, process, lien,* or *debt*, along with a host of other negative words, will undoubtedly come up. The fact of the matter is a mortgage can be defined in one very simple and positive word—MONEY. That's it.

A mortgage is a *monetary* transaction, nothing more. We apply for a mortgage loan because we need (or want) *money*. Whether we are buying a house, refinancing a mortgage, consolidating debts, or getting cash for important life purposes, we need *money*. Think of it this way: The first step in a mortgage transaction is the application (asking for money) and the last step in the mortgage transaction is disbursement (getting the money). So if the beginning is money and the end is money, then the product must be money! Why is this important to you, as a borrower? Because it makes a mortgage a monetary transaction, making it easy to identify both the benefits and costs of the loan to determine the true value. This is a tried and true concept in determining whether a loan benefits you.

A Mortgage Formula for Success

What has happened in recent years should not have happened. Significant events in the mortgage markets and banking industry have had major repercussions on consumers and homeowners. The time to empower you to take back control of your mortgage is now!

I worked in a mortgage market that between 1983 and 2000 was fairly conservative. For twenty-five years I have believed in the idea that, as mortgage professionals, our primary responsibility is to offer our customers a loan that provides life-changing benefits. My formula for success was simple: *Help borrowers who have the equity and income to qualify, protect each borrower with a loan that truly makes sense, and offer a loan that* improves their situation and life in every way possible. It was that simple then and it is still that simple today. Unfortunately, many in the mortgage industry seem to have moved away from this approach. Therefore, this book is designed to equip you with the knowledge to be able to accomplish this formula on your own.

Navigating the Mortgage Maze is more than just a formula or how-to guide. It will reveal many truths about mortgages, debt, and financing that most consumers have never learned —truths that, if applied, can set you on a path for financial independence.

A Mortgage Is an Investment!

Here is just one of those truths. Most of us think of a mortgage as simply a very large debt. But in fact, *a mortgage is really an investment*—most likely the biggest investment you will ever make in your lifetime! It is the vehicle that allows you to eventually own the biggest asset you have—your home! But homeownership is costly. Between the mortgage payment, taxes, insurance, improvements, utilities, and upkeep, it is a huge investment. And as with any investment, if you are going to put that much in, you want to get something in return! For that reason, it is an investment that needs to be made wisely.

I mentioned earlier that I will give you timeless truths in this book to support many of the concepts I will teach you. To get you thinking about the importance of handling your investments wisely, consider this story from Jesus of Nazareth recorded in the Bible. This great teacher told a parable of a businessman who gave three of his servants money to invest while he was away on an extended business trip. When the man returned he praised and rewarded the first two for multiplying their amounts. But he scolded the third, who simply hid the money in the ground out of fear for what the man would do to him if he lost it. Then the businessman took it from him and gave it to the servant who had done the best with his money.

Jesus applied the story this way: "To those who use well what they are given, even more will be given, and they will have an abundance. But from those who do nothing, even what little they have will be taken away."[3]

There is a great principle to be learned here. We want to do the most with the money we invest—and there is none bigger than our home—and not make decisions that could squander our equity or put us in a position where we could lose it. If we make wise choices with our home, our equity, our debt, and our finances, which I will teach you how to do throughout this book, we will eventually have an abundance.

This only happens when we have a well-thought-out strategy and long-term plan. But if we waste our equity, overburden ourselves with debt, or misuse our finances, what we have been given we could ultimately lose. My hope for you is that, after reading this book, you will never be a victim of that in the future!

After all, you have worked hard for your home. Your home is also a gift—a gift from God.[4] If you had been born in a country like India, where in many areas the daily wages are fifty cents to one dollar per day, you could have easily worked just as hard as you do now and yet never owned a home. The fact that we live in a great country where we have the opportunity to earn enough income to own a home and all the other things we are blessed with is certainly a gift from God! Now let me help you to do the best with what you have.

Your financial well-being touches nearly every aspect of your life: work, marriage, family, faith, relationships, emotional and physical health, attitude, and overall happiness. Because I want to help you go beyond financial success to achieve life success, I have included nuggets of wisdom and biblical perspectives that can have a powerful impact on your life and your future in significant, and possibly even eternal, ways. The final chapter, "Moving to Real Life Change," addresses real life change and how you can create a legacy in many areas of your life.

My hope, then, is that this book leaves you a changed person with a new outlook on your mortgage, your finances, your life, and your legacy.

NOTES

1. Stephanie Armour, "Foreclosures Take an Emotional Toll on Many Homeowners, *USA Today*, May 14, 2008.
2. Ibid.
3. Matthew 25:15–29.
4. The Bible says all good things come from God: "Whatever is good and perfect comes down to us from God our Father, who created all the lights in the heavens. He never changes or casts a shifting shadow" (James 1:17).

CHAPTER ONE

THE TOP 10 MORTGAGE
Traps

Obtaining a mortgage creates the opportunity of home-ownership and all that goes with it: your own home, solid equity, a growing investment, even tax savings. But getting a mortgage can also be a complex and confusing process that includes obstacles and challenges, not unlike running a maze.

How do you navigate the mortgage maze? By having a map that helps you become aware of all the turns and sharp corners—those mistakes most first-time and repeat mortgage buyers make when they go to finance or refinance their home. Let's begin the process by looking at the top 10 mortgage mistakes homeowners make that get them caught in the traps.

Mistake #1: Making Rate the #1 Consideration

The Brunsons bought their home in the eighties when interest rates were high. They started with a 10 percent, thirty-year mortgage. Every time rates dropped, they refinanced. They just completed their eighth refinance and are down to a 5.0 percent interest rate, lower than any rate in the market! The Brunsons feel they have managed their mortgage very well and have saved themselves tens of thousands of dollars in payments over the years through the many rate reductions. Unfortunately, the Brunsons have actually lost hundreds of thousands of dollars without even knowing it. You see, although they have reduced their rate eight times, they have also extended their term eight times, paid fees eight times, and decreased their taxes eight times! The result: they have been paying for twenty-four years on their home, owe more today than they have ever owed, and are no closer to being debt free . . . and retirement is twenty-four years closer than when they got their first mortgage! Although the Brunsons have the lowest rate they have ever had, they are in the worst position they have ever been!

Does the Brunsons' story sound familiar to you? Have you been a homeowner for several years and made this same mistake? How did this happen? We typically put our primary focus on interest rate and miss out on the *real benefits* of mortgage financing. It is the first question we generally ask and the one we put the most weight on when determining whether the loan is a "good deal." *Believe it or not, the interest rate on a mortgage loan* is not *the number one consideration!* For years I have taught mortgage professionals a simple concept: *Rate Doesn't Matter.*

I realize this sounds radical and ridiculous when you first hear it, but I will prove this concept to you throughout this book. In the mainstream media and by most mortgage loan officers, all we have ever been told is that *rate matters!* We have been programmed that *rate is the primary consideration* when borrowing—nothing is more important. That is not completely true. The truth is, when finding a mortgage loan that has true financial value, lasting monetary benefits, and good overall financial sense, the interest rate, although important, is only one of numerous criteria to consider—many of the others being equally or more important to the overall cost and benefits of the loan.

DID YOU KNOW?

A Good Faith Estimate (GFE) is just that—an estimate. It is not required to tell you what the *actual* rates, terms, fees, costs, and APR are going to be for the mortgage you *ultimately* get. Additionally, the GFEs are usually sent before the income is verified, appraisal is completed, and title is received. Changes in any of these could significantly change the terms of the mortgage loan the borrower was originally quoted. Many companies do not send a second GFE after final approval and, therefore, the borrower never sees the changes until the closing.

In most mortgage transactions, several considerations outweigh the interest rate—factors we will discuss and educate you on in detail. But for now, let me share with you a little-known fact:

◇◇◇

**The rate you get on a mortgage loan
is almost never the rate you actually pay.**

◇◇◇

Mistake #2: The Payment Reduction Trap

The Williamses have decided to refinance their home to pay off their debts and reduce their payments. The bills have been mounting and they have come to the realization that they cannot afford their current payments comfortably. They max out their equity and consolidate several credit cards, an auto loan, a student loan, and their current mortgage into a new thirty-year loan. In doing so, they reduce their current total payments by $700 per month! They are pleased with their new payment and think they have really helped themselves.

One year later they realize they actually put themselves in worse financial shape. Not only did they use the credit cards and run the balances right back up to the limits again, but because they had a free and clear title on the car they decided to use it to buy a new one. They thought they could afford it with their $700 payment reduction. In addition, to accomplish the lower payments while increasing the loan balance, they extended the term of the loan by five years when they refinanced. As a result, their overall debt and payments are now the highest they have ever been.

Most important, their consolidation loan did nothing in solving the real cause for their debt—their spending habits. Now they have less available cash and more debt, and they are further from a free and clear home than ever before!

This is the most common dilemma I have seen in my years in the mortgage business. This is a critical mistake that has destroyed marriages and homes. In our desire to improve our situation for the immediate future, we end up compromising our long-term security. Consolidating debt into a mortgage loan *can be* an effective and powerful way to use your home's equity if done correctly. However, when done incorrectly, it has devastating effects.

The primary mistake the Williamses made in consolidating their debts was putting too much focus on payment reduction. The extra cash flow they achieved created a false sense of security and led to their cre-

DID YOU KNOW?

Many borrowers pay more in costs and fees for their mortgage loan in the first few years than they gain in savings and benefits.

ating *new* debt. This also led to a five-year extension on their mortgage and dozens of years on their consumer debt. In other words, they increased both the amount and the length of their debt—two critical mistakes—all in the name of payment reduction. They never had a long-term financial plan in place to get out of debt or to own their home free and clear. Finally, they never sought counsel on managing their budget and spending habits to avoid getting back into trouble with their debt.

A proper consolidation loan can actually lead to debt reduction, term reduction, tax reduction, and substantial savings both short- and long-term. This kind of borrowing, combined with the proper budgeting, can lead to debt-free and financially astute living. This should be our ultimate goal with any mortgage transaction! The Bible says it best in Romans 13:8: "Owe nothing to anyone—except for your obligation to love one another." Now that would be a life worth living!

<><><>

Our primary objective in every mortgage transaction should be to borrow in a way that reduces debt, improves financial stability, and helps us get debt free in as short a time as possible!

<><><>

Mistake #3: Focusing on Short-term Gain

Millions of unsuspecting borrowers between 2004 and 2006 purchased or refinanced homes during the mortgage "boom" at high loan to values (loan amounts that exceeded 90 percent of the customer's property value), when interest rates had reached all-time lows, property values had reached all-time highs, and lending programs were the most aggressive in U.S. history. Many of these borrowers, in an attempt to capitalize on the lowest possible interest rates, financed their loans through adjustable rate mortgages (ARMs) or "option-arm" mortgages with attractive rates that were fixed for only two- or three-year initial terms or had interest-only options.

In addition, many borrowed against their growing equity to get cash for short-term purposes. Unfortunately, the higher rate adjustments for those ARMs came during the mortgage and real estate "bust" that began in late 2006 and continued for more than two years, as interest rates escalated, property values plummeted, and availability of high loan-to-value programs evaporated. The result: Borrowers faced significant payment increases, and they could neither afford the higher payments nor obtain new financing to correct the situation. As of this writing, many homeowners are struggling through this situation, and some have even lost their homes in the process.

The soaring foreclosures in 2007 and 2008—foreclosure filings jumped 75 percent[1] from April 2007 to April 2008— teach us that getting a mortgage for short-term gain with no regard for the long-term impact can be a devastating mistake! Most of us tend to look only at our short-term needs and situation when financing. As a result, we go into a mortgage transaction with a single thought in mind—solve today's problem or take advantage of today's opportunities. How many of these thoughts enter your mind or lips when borrowing?

- "*Right now* I just need to focus on lowering my monthly payment(s) so I can pay my bills."
- "Wow, rates are really low on adjustable rate mortgages, so I think I'll go with that *for now* and refinance to a fixed rate later."

- "I just want to pay off those creditors *as soon as possible* so I can get them off my back."
- "I want my dream home *now*."
- "I just need to make sure my payments don't exceed $1,500, because that's all I can afford *today*."

When we go into a mortgage transaction with this kind of short-term mind-set, we make costly mistakes. Focusing only on the short term puts us in a position to make bad choices. We ignore all other factors that lead to the *overall value* of the loan in order to achieve that one singular goal now—whether the goal is a lower payment, a lower interest rate, or a dream home. In the long term, this always proves to be costly.

Mistake #4: Missing the "Big Picture about Debt"

The Ahmads are considering a mortgage refinance. They have over $30,000 in consumer debt, but do not want to include it in any refinancing because it is "personal" debt, not mortgage debt. They plan to pay off the debt balances with the payment savings they will receive from their mortgage refinance. They refinance their existing thirty-year mortgage to a new thirty-year mortgage and reduce their payments by $200 per month. Three years later they have even more consumer debt than when they originally refinanced. The money they saved just never made its way to pay off the consumer debt. So much for their plan . . .

Have you been struggling with making payments on your debt for years and have had the equity to pay it off but just never felt it was the right thing to do? If so, you are like the Ahmads and many other families. We tend to compartmentalize our debt: categorizing our mortgage debt as one kind of debt, installment loans as another, and credit cards as still another. Most treat all personal (consumer) debt separately from mortgage debt. The fact is that *debt is debt.* All of it is owed and has to be paid back!

DID YOU KNOW?

According to *BusinessWeek*, U.S. households in 2008 owed almost $14 trillion, nearly equal to the annual output of the U.S. economy. According to the Federal Reserve Statistical Release on Consumer Credit, as of August 7, 2008, revolving debt increased at an annual rate of 7.4 percent in 2008 compared to 2.9 percent in 2003. In addition, "credit-card debt has been growing much faster than the economy—more than 8 percent in the final two quarters of 2007 and over 7 percent in May, 2008."[2]

King Solomon addressed this situation in Proverbs 22:7 by saying, "Just as the rich rule the poor, so the borrower is the servant to the lender."

Did you know that through a mortgage loan you may actually be able to use your personal debt to eliminate all of your debt faster? Did you know that in many cases credit card debt is as long in term as many mortgages? Although debt is a "bad" thing, as a homeowner *with equity*, it can temporarily be a good thing, because it provides a means to actually leverage your payments and convert them into a far greater financial position. This is done by taking the high payments you are making on your existing debt, including your personal debt, and converting them into a mortgage loan that can create reductions in payment, term, and taxes, and possibly provide additional cash. We will teach you how to do this in detail later in this book. The key is in knowing how to borrow properly.

◇◇◇

Debt, when properly leveraged, can be converted directly into payment reduction, additional cash, increased tax deductibility, and term reduction with little or no initial cost!

◇◇◇

Mistake #5: The Equity Asset Trap

Mr. Jones has a $300,000 home with a $175,000 mortgage. He is looking to refinance his mortgage to a lower rate in order to lower his payments. He also would like to get $10,000 to complete some important improvements around the house. Mr. Jones qualifies for a loan that allows him to borrow up to 80 percent of his home's equity, which means he could get up to $65,000 cash. However, he wants to retain his equity as a safety net in case something unforeseen happens, so he only borrows the minimum of what he needs.

A year later, Mr. Jones loses his job. He is given only thirty days' pay and has no other job prospects. Six months later he is still out of work. He is financially strapped and behind on all of his bills. If only he had some cash in reserve! He has lots of equity in his home, but no way to access it because he cannot qualify for a mortgage loan in his current state. The only possible way he can get out of this situation now is to sell his dream home. Unfortunately, if he does so, not only does he have to uproot his family, but he still will not qualify for a loan to buy a new one.

If he had utilized his equity during his refinance and drawn out cash for investment, he would have had access to the cash as an emergency fund to get him through until the house sold. Unfortunately, all that equity is doing him little good right now.

Our home is the greatest asset that most of us will ever have. Our home's equity is what I refer to as our "hidden savings account." It is an asset that, if used properly, can be converted into cash for sound purposes. However, many people never take advantage of that opportunity. They treat their equity as a dormant asset just sitting there for a "rainy day." The fact is that your equity is here today, but can be gone tomorrow, as is evident in the cyclical increases—and decreases—in home values in the past decade (and even earlier). The problem with the declines in property values is they remove equity from homeowners—and once you lose equity you may not get it all back. Let me give you an analogy about a stock investment to really bring this point home.

DID YOU KNOW?

In the U.S. Census Bureau and Department of Housing and Urban Development's *Current Housing Reports for 2005*, it was estimated that there were 74,931,000 owner-occupied single-family homes in the United States. Of those, 24,776,000 (33 percent) were free and clear homes. Based on a median sales price of $240,900 in 2005, that represented 5.9 trillion dollars in unused equity from those homes alone.

Let's say you have stock in an investment account valued at $50,000 today. What's your stock's worth? You are probably thinking, *That's a dumb question—it's worth $50,000!* Actually, it's not! It is a stock—so it has value only on paper.

In the real world it has real value only when you convert it to cash and make it a liquid asset. . . . It's worth nothing until you cash it in!

Equity works exactly the same way—your equity is worth nothing to you until you access it. To convert it from its dormant asset state to a *liquid asset* you have to "cash it in." This is a principle the majority of people miss and one we will discuss in great detail. There are two key principles when cashing in your equity:

1. Only cash in your equity for sound investment purposes with proper direction and advice, in conservative investments that protect the cash (and your equity).
2. Borrow in a way that allows you to reduce the balance on your mortgage faster so as to reestablish your equity and eliminate your debt at the same time.

Although these two rules appear to be at odds with each other, you can accomplish both if you borrow properly.

◇◇◇

When used properly and financed correctly, your home's equity can be used to achieve major life goals, such as college funding and retirement, while both offsetting the interest costs and accelerating the term reduction.

◇◇◇

Mistake #6: Term at All Costs (The Perpetual Mortgage Treadmill)

Mr. and Mrs. Fielder have lived in five homes over the past twenty-five years. They have refinanced their mortgages several times over those years to access the benefits of lower interest and payments. Unfortunately, all that money they saved was spent on frivolous things that mean nothing today. Mr. and Mrs. Fielder just bought the home where they plan to spend their retirement. They are both fifty-five and had planned to retire at age sixty.

There is just one problem—without really thinking about it, Mr. and Mrs. Fielder took out another thirty-year mortgage and now realize they will be unable to afford their mortgage payments based on their future reduced retirement income.

The Fielders do the math: They have paid over $700,000 in mortgage payments over their lifetime and still have over $400,000 in future mortgage payments on their new mortgage. Not only have they spent their retirement earnings on mortgage payments, they have no hope of being debt free during their retirement years without selling their home and moving into a small one-bedroom apartment. Their plan of *retiring at age sixty is looking dismal.*

Most borrowers tend to gravitate toward the thirty-year mortgage term, just as the Fielders did. In fact, the majority of mortgage transactions are based on thirty-year amortizations—87 percent of all fixed-rate, fixed-term mortgages were thirty-year terms or longer in 2007 (according to the Mortgage Bankers Association annual mortgage origination survey). Only 6.1 percent were fifteen-year terms. What is even more perplexing is that the median age of first-time home buyers was thirty-two years old (according to the 2006 National Association of Realtors® Profile of Home Buyers and Sellers). At the young age of thirty-two, retirement is not much of a consideration, but when considering a thirty-year transaction it should be.

Significantly, the median age of refinance borrowers is even higher, likely over age forty. Recognizing that 87 percent of all fixed-term mortgages are for thirty years or more, most of these fortysomethings are committing to overly long terms. In thirty years, when they finally pay off their home, they will be in their seventies—most likely past their planned retirement. For some reason, when we borrow on a mortgage, we seem to have blinders on and choose a term that in no way meets our long-term retirement objectives.

The mistake here is that we do not borrow with a *future cost mind-set or a debt elimination date* (DED; see chapter 7). As a result, many of us unknowingly spend our retirement on mortgage payments! It is imperative we put more emphasis on the term. We want to enjoy our "golden years" and live a comfortable lifestyle, so we need to be sure we are positioning ourselves to be debt free. We must understand that for many of us our current income, which usually increases annually, will most likely reduce at retirement and convert to a fixed income for the remainder of our lives.

> **DID YOU KNOW?**
>
> From 1991 to 2007, the rate of personal bankruptcy filings among those ages 65 or older jumped by 150 percent, according to AARP. . . . The most startling rise occurred among those ages 75 to 84, whose rate soared 433 percent.[3]

◇◇◇

Mortgage financing is a critical part of your retirement strategy. Smart financing can possibly lead you to owning your home free and clear at your desired retirement age and provide you with a substantial asset!

◇◇◇

Mistake #7: Underutilizing the Tax Potential

The Hendersons were very happy with their new mortgage refinance, the rate they received, and the lower payment. They thanked their mortgage counselor for all her help. The next year they completed their taxes and discovered their tax deductions for mortgage interest had declined substantially. Once they figured out the increase in taxes, they realized that they had given almost one-third of their payment savings back to the government!

When was the last time you worked with a mortgage loan officer who completely explained the tax ramifications and impact of your mortgage loan? Most loan officers, as well as consumers, do not understand the tax implications of mortgage financing (and as a result completely miss opportunities to reduce taxes), but more painfully, usually *increase* federal taxes with a mortgage refinance. That was the sad scenario for the Hendersons.

One of the primary benefits to mortgage financing—and one of the primary reasons you

D I D   Y O U   K N O W ?

When you refinance to a lower rate, with no cash out or debt consolidation, you may end up paying more in income taxes. As a result, you may give back more than 25 percent of the payment savings you gained in the first year alone.

would choose to borrow against your home instead of on an unsecured basis—is the tax advantage. Did you know that the tax benefits of a mortgage loan can actually reduce your effective interest rate and provide you thousands in additional savings if done properly? The key is knowing and understanding the tax benefits and ramifications of a mortgage loan. This is another critical aspect of the overall cost and savings associated with mortgage financing.

◇◇◇

By understanding and capitalizing on the tax benefits of mortgage financing, you can not only avoid tax increases that are common with mortgage financing, but substantially decrease the amount of taxes you pay annually!

◇◇◇

Mistake #8: Confusing Interest Rates with APRs

Ms. Patel has been working with a loan officer on her mortgage loan for two weeks now. She has been told all along that her interest rate is 6.50 percent. Today she is at the closing and the loan documents show an annual percentage rate (APR) of 7.16 percent. What happened?

Many borrowers have experienced this dilemma. The APR typically exceeds the posted rate because of fees added to the loan as part of processing and closing costs. Interest rates and APRs are two different numbers on a mortgage loan in all cases, *except* a no-cost, no-fee, or no-point loan (which rarely exists) or when all the fees are prepaid (which rarely happens). For millions, the rate they are actually paying is higher than the rate they think they are getting. You need to know this, because it directly affects what you *actually* pay for a mortgage loan.

DID YOU KNOW?

The APR calculation was established by the federal government's 1968 Truth in Lending Act to help borrowers understand the true cost of their loan. The intention was to create a simple indicator to help compare loan offers between different companies and protect consumers from being taken advantage of or fooled. The reasons for the APR calculation were all good. Unfortunately, the reality is that it has not accomplished its purpose. The vast majority of consumers do not understand and are confused by the APR.

Although there are many ethical mortgage professionals in the marketplace, unethical loan officers and mortgage originators play "the rate game." They use semantics, confusing jargon, complex words, misrepresentation, and incomplete or nondisclosure to confuse borrowers. You do not need to be a victim of this. To get the best rate possible, you need to know how to determine the *real* rate—the APR that shows the annualized interest cost of the mortgage.

◇◇◇

Understanding the difference between interest rates and APRs allows you to confidently determine the true cost of your loan and accurately compare offers between companies.

◇◇◇

Mistake #9: Paying Unnecessary and Hidden Fees

Mr. Chin is at his loan closing and has just found several fees he knew nothing about. The loan officer claims he told him about them, but Mr. Chin is certain he did not. His only choices are to walk away and start over, or "bite the bullet" and close.

Because he has already made commitments based on the money he is receiving at closing, he begrudgingly closes the loan. He will never buy from that loan officer, or that company, again!

Has that ever happened to you? Let me run a few common mortgage terminologies by you. Do you know what a "discount point" is? Sounds like you're getting a deal, doesn't it? Hardly! How about a "Yield Spread Premium" (YSP)? "Junk fee"? "Pre-payment penalty"? If these all sound foreign, don't feel alone!

Paying unnecessary or hidden fees is a common mistake that does not need to be made. Millions of people have purchased "no cost" mortgage loans that had all kinds of costs. Millions more have gone to closing to find out about fees they never knew existed or were hidden. In fact, many times the unsuspecting, uninformed, and uneducated customer never finds out until the day of closing. By that point, they simply do not want to start over and just want to get their money. As a result, they close and chalk it up to experience (only for it to happen again). Not only are loan documents, and the disclosures that reveal the fees and costs, confusing, but the loan officer may not completely explain all the fees.

The fact is that with a simple financial calculator, the educated borrower can check the loan officer's figures and know the fees and costs before the closing. No more surprises or disappointments! And knowing the exact costs and fees of a mortgage loan can help us negotiate the best deal possible.

Mistake #10: Comparing Mortgage Products That Are Incomparable

The Andersons spent three weeks negotiating a mortgage loan. During the process they worked with four different mortgage companies. They even went through an Internet lender service. All four offered them something different. They finally chose the company they felt had the best rate and terms for what they were looking for. They did not end up getting as much cash as they wanted or paying off all the debts they had hoped to, and they paid a little higher interest rate and fees than they had expected. In addition, they ended up with an adjustable-rate loan instead of the fixed-rate loan they had originally asked for. But they still felt they got a pretty good deal. After all, the loan officer seemed knowledgeable and said this was the best deal out there, and it did seem to be the best of the four.

A week after closing their loan, they ran into an old friend at a party who happens to be in the mortgage industry. After telling him about their new loan they come to find out that there were much better programs out there that could have done everything they wanted. They could have saved and gotten so much more!

Almost no one, when applying for a mortgage loan, simply buys from the first person they talk to, unless it is a loan officer they previously worked with. Even that can be a mistake. We all "shop" for a mortgage to compare rates. The reason—to make sure we get the best deal. However, because we really do not know the right way to shop and compare mortgages, rarely do we actually end up getting the best deal. There are thousands of companies and programs out there, all with different products, parameters, and processes. Unfortunately, when we compare we are many times comparing apples to bananas!

Many times we compare loans and loan products that look nothing alike. We get confused by all of the different programs.

The mistake is that we did not go in with a clear understanding of exactly what we wanted and did not know how to shop properly.

Because our primary focus is on getting the lowest interest rate (the number one mistake), we either miss the most important characteristics of different loans or get taken advantage of

> **D I D   Y O U   K N O W ?**
>
> There are thousands of mortgage providers and nearly every one delivers and provides their products, programs, and processes differently.

by someone who knows how to play the rate game. The fact is that in order to shop and compare we must know how to put different lenders on the same playing field. We must compare common products and characteristics. To do so, we must apply a simple law of science: To prove the facts, you must test like scenarios and remove any variables.

Now that we have discussed the most common mistakes made in mortgage financing (many of which I am certain you can relate to), I will spend the rest of this book educating and empowering you to not only avoid these mistakes, but take complete control of your mortgage and future!

NOTES

1. Irvine, California based REALTYTRAC, Inc., as reported in Stephanie Armour, "Foreclosures Take an Emotional Toll on Many Homeowners," *USA Today*, May 14, 2008.

2. Geoff Colvin, "The Next Credit Crunch," *Fortune*, August 18, 2008, as cited at www.money.cnn.com/2008/08/18/news/economy/Colvin_next_credit_crunch.fortune/index.htm.

3. Also reported in *USA Today* June 16, 2008. The findings come from research by the Consumer Bankruptcy Project.

CHAPTER TWO

IS IT REALLY ALL ABOUT
Rate?

It's time to debunk decades-old conventional wisdom and flawed, but generally accepted views surrounding interest rates and annual percentage rates (APRs). Interest rates are the most common central focus of mortgage financing, and we tend to put all of our eggs in the "interest rate basket." This is a critical mistake—mistake #1 in the opening chapter. There's a lot more to interest rates than meets the eye. Remember:

◇◇◇

Interest rates are not the most important consideration in a mortgage transaction!

◇◇◇

As you will learn, what you see is almost never what you get. By understanding interest rates and annual percentage rates in simple terms, you will be empowered to master the most confusing part of the mortgage transaction.

Let me share a foundational truth for any kind of purchase, including a mortgage:

◇◇◇

**Price is what you *pay*. Value is what you *get*.
It's *never* what you pay that matters, but *always* what you get!**

◇◇◇

If you really think about this statement, you will find it to be true in *all* cases, for *all* products, and *all* services. Consider these questions:

1. Have you ever bought something, paid more for it, and got more value?
2. Have you ever bought something, paid more for it, and got less value?
3. Have you ever bought something, paid more for it, and got the same value?

I am confident that your answer to all three of these questions was yes. We have all done it. What do these questions prove? They prove that *price and value are separate elements in all purchases.*

Price and value are simply two different things. One does not ensure the other. Paying more for a product or service does not necessarily *get* you more; it just means you *paid* more. The same holds true for a mortgage. And the inverse, paying less, does not mean you get more; it just means you paid less. Let's look at it another way.

Let's make this specific to a mortgage transaction by replacing "price" with "rates, points, and fees" (the three primary price elements of a mortgage loan) and "value" with "money":

◇◇◇

Rates, points, and fees are what you *pay*. Money is what you *get*. It's *never* what you pay that matters, but *always* what you get!

◇◇◇

We tend to look for the lowest rate, but what we really are looking for is the best loan possible, at the lowest rate possible, that helps us pay the least and get the most. In a mortgage transaction, this means getting the most benefit for your loan. In later chapters, I will reveal four major benefits that will change your entire thinking about mortgage loans. But first, let's try to understand interest rates and APRs and their role in the mortgage transaction.

Understanding APR: Is It Really Truth in Lending?

Have you ever been confused by the fact that the interest rate and annual percentage rate on your mortgage documents are usually two different numbers? Ever gone to a loan closing to find that the APR was different from the interest rate you were quoted and no one could explain to you why? Ever wondered what APR *really means* and *really is?* If your answer is yes to any of these, you are no different from

> **DID YOU KNOW?**
>
> When searching "Web Definitions of APR" on Google, I found twenty-seven different definitions. No wonder the vast majority of consumers do not understand APR.

millions of others who have experienced the same confusion. This is not surprising, considering that much of the information out there on APRs from reputable sources is confusing and conflicting.

As noted earlier ("Did You Know," p. 36) the APR calculation was established to help borrowers understand the true cost of their loan by comparing loan offers among different companies. The APR can effectively do this only if you are comparing two loans with identical components. Unfortunately, that often does not happen because loan offers are usually different between lenders. This removes any basis for equal comparison. The reasons for creating the APR calculation were all good. Unfortunately, the reality is that it has not accomplished its objective. As consumers, the Truth in Lending Act should give us comfort to know that there is "truth" in lending. However, many of us have had a far different experience!

To help you understand APRs and take full advantage of the purposes for which they were created, let's begin by discussing the terms *APR* and *interest rate*. Many times we refer to these terms as if they are interchangeable. The fact is that the APR and interest rate are usually two different things in a mortgage transaction. It is important to understand the difference between the two because they can help you in determining the *actual cost* and *lowest cost* when comparing loans.

◇◇◇

APR is the actual interest paid for the *amount financed* annually, based on the monthly payment and the loan term.

◇◇◇

The key term in this definition is *amount financed*. Today's Truth in Lending disclosures use two terms on the form: *amount financed* and *loan amount*:

1. The amount financed is the amount you actually *borrow before* the costs and fees. Simplified: it is the amount of *money* you actually get.

2. The loan amount is the amount you actually *owe after* including the costs and fees financed in the loan. Simplified: it is the amount of *debt* you actually borrow.

D I D   Y O U   K N O W ?

A mortgage calculator is a standard tool used to determine mortgage loan payments that every consumer *must* consult before entering into a mortgage transaction. You can find it on the Web sites of many financial institutions (including most banks as part of their resources when considering a mortgage) as well as at my Web site at www.mortgagempowered.com; a loan calculator is also included in the Microsoft Excel software. A loan calculator will prevent dishonesty, because a calculator never lies! By having a financial calculator to test the validity of the numbers, you will save yourself hundreds, if not thousands, of dollars.

There are only four factors that go into any mortgage loan calculation: *loan amount, interest rate, term,* and *payment*. Any three factors, when entered, will compute the fourth. Doing such calculations form a critical step to understanding, determining, and validating the lowest cost and best loan for you and your family.

◇◇◇

Therefore, the loan amount is the amount financed plus all fees and costs financed into the loan.

◇◇◇

In mortgage transactions it is commonplace to finance fees and costs as part of the loan. This can work to your advantage if you want to keep the out-of-pocket costs low when borrowing, as it keeps you from having to pay them at closing. This also can lead to the costs and fees being tax deductible, as they may become (in some cases) a form of prepaid interest. It is important to always consult a certified tax advisor whenever borrowing on a mortgage loan. The downside to financing your fees and costs is that you end up paying additional interest because these fees are financed in the loan over the term. By doing this, it changes the *effective* interest rate for the loan because the loan amount and monthly payment increase to compensate for the fees. This increase in payment, in turn, changes the *actual cost* of the loan when compared to the amount financed. This is the primary cause of the APR and interest rate being different.

The interest rate and the APR are exactly the same in only one circumstance: when there are absolutely no fees, costs, or points financed in the loan (which rarely happens)—in other words, when the amount financed and the loan amount are the same. In this case there is no change in payment.

To better understand this, let's look at two scenarios.

Scenario #1 (No Fees Included). You borrow $100,000 (your amount financed) at a fixed interest rate of 6.0 percent for thirty years. There are no loan fees (or the fees were paid up front by you). Because there are no additional costs financed into the loan, the $100,000 *amount financed* is also the *loan amount.* Based on the amount financed, term, and interest rate, your payment is $599.55. Because the amount financed and loan amount are the same, your interest rate and APR are both exactly 6.0 percent.

Scenario #2 (Fees Included). You borrow the same $100,000 (amount financed). But this time you finance $2,000 in loan fees and closing costs into the loan. This makes your loan amount $102,000—the original amount financed plus the loan fees. The interest rate is still 6.0 percent on the loan. However, the APR for the loan is now 6.19 percent, and the payment increases to $611.54. Why? Because the new APR and payment reflect the fees you financed in the loan. The APR changes because, as we defined earlier, APR is the actual interest paid for the amount financed, annually, based on the monthly payment and the loan term. The payment went up because you are financing $2,000 in fees as part of the larger loan amount. Therefore, because your payment went up in comparison to your amount financed, your APR reflects the increase.

You can use a mortgage calculator to clarify this. Enter the *amount financed,* $100,000; the monthly payment, $611.54; and the term, thirty years. The APR comes out to 6.19 percent. To reflect the true cost of the $100,000 amount financed based on this $11.54 increase (the cost of the additional fees), an additional .19 percent has been added to the interest rate.

The interest rate changed to reflect the new payment, which included the fees, for the thirty-year term calculated on the amount financed (the actual cash you received).

Let me sum all this up with one defining statement:

◇◇◇

The APR is *always* based on the amount financed,
and the interest rate is *always* based on the loan amount.
Only when there are no fees are the APR and
interest rate the same.

◇◇◇

Now that you understand the difference between interest rate and APR and how they work, you should never be confused or fooled again! The key is being able to calculate the loan terms to ensure that the rate you are actually getting is the one you were quoted.

What Is Rate's Role in a Mortgage Transaction?

We've said it many times: Rate is *not* the number one consideration in a mortgage loan. So what is rate's role in a mortgage transaction? Recall the four *factors* that go into any mort-gage loan calculation: the rate, the payment, the loan amount, and the term. Only three of these are actual *components* of the loan itself. Can you name them? Here is the answer:

1. The loan amount (the cash)
2. The payment (the cost)
3. The term (the payback)

Notice something *interesting* here (no pun intended!): Rate *is not* a component of the loan. Think of it this way: When you get a mortgage loan, you do not *get* a rate, you *pay* a rate. You *get* money (loan amount) for a specified period of time (term) at a specified monthly cost (payment). That's all you get! So what is rate's role in the equation? Rate affects one, and only one, component: *payment*. It does not affect the loan amount or the term. In other words, rate is a factor of the *payment*. Let's take that a step further.

Everyone makes rate the number one criteria and prior-ity when borrowing. It is all we have ever heard about when it comes to loans. Experts, financial counselors, and the media tell us that *rate is king*. Therefore, we focus on rate first because we do not know what else to focus on. The fact is there are much more important criteria to getting a mortgage loan with true intrinsic value. Rate is only one of many factors that go into a truly beneficial mortgage loan. The primary reason we look for the lowest rate is to save the most money. However, many of the factors outside of rate ultimately dictate how much we will save, how much we will get, and how much the loan will cost.

Remember what we established in the opening pages of this

book: *a mortgage is money*. Our ultimate goal is to not only *save* the most, but also *get* the most, *both at the same time*! Now that would make for a *truly valuable loan*!

The "Lowest Rate" Virtually Does Not Exist!

When getting a mortgage loan, every one of us looks for the lowest rate. This is one of the biggest misconceptions out there. Did you realize that actually getting the "lowest rate" is nearly impossible? I am sure you are wondering how that can be. Think about this: Hundreds of lenders are out there. How many of them have the *lowest* rate? Only one—that is why they are called the lowest. To get the lowest rate, you would literally have to find the lender with the lowest rate in the entire world! Unfortunately, there are three problems with finding that one lender:

- *"Lowest Rate" Problem 1*: Nobody I have ever met knows who the lowest rate lender is. Many claim to be the lowest, but that is almost never true! Why? Because of problem 2.
- *"Lowest Rate" Problem 2*: There are hundreds of lending sources in the United States alone. To find the lowest rate, you would have to compare all of them. Even with the advent of technology and the World Wide Web, this is impossible. In fact, when I Googled "Mortgage Loan Providers," there were 3,520,000 pages! When I Googled "Lowest Rate Mortgage Loan," there were 2,220,000 pages! Who has the time or patience to do this much research in today's busy lifestyle? Even if we did, we would still be faced with problem 3.

• *"Lowest Rate" Problem 3*: By the time we found the lowest rate lender, they would no longer be the lowest, because *rates change constantly*!

The fact is, getting the lowest rate is nearly impossible! If you happened to stumble upon the lowest rate it would be only by chance, not purpose. Frankly, most lenders are within one-eighth to one-quarter percent of one another for similar mortgage products. The difference in payments between two lenders that are .25 percent apart can be a minimal cost in comparison to the differences you might find between those same lenders in the overall costs of the loan. Therefore, trying to find the lowest rate is not only futile, but it does not ensure the best loan anyway!

Although getting the lowest rate may be impossible, getting a low, competitive rate is very easy to do. In chapter 9, we will teach you how to shop in a way to ensure that you pay among the lowest possible rates for your situation every time. We will also show you, throughout this book, how the loan with a little higher rate sometimes offers much better benefits and savings in both the short and long term. To place all your effort and energy into rate alone, when there are so many other factors (some that outweigh rate), would not maximize your time.

Let's address further misconceptions about interest rates.

Rate Isn't the Primary Consideration

Yes, you read that correctly: "Rate Isn't the Primary Consideration," except in one case. So what is that one case where rate is the primary consideration?

◇◇◇

Rate is the primary consideration only when you are comparing two otherwise identical loan offers with identical characteristics that do exactly the same thing. Only then does a lower rate directly equate to a better loan.

◇◇◇

The truth is that this scenario is uncommon among most borrowers because they do not compare exact mortgages. In the majority of cases, customers are looking at loans from different lenders with different components and different criteria.

None of this is to say that rate is not a critically important factor and consideration when borrowing, because it is.

Still, the interest rate on a mortgage, in and of itself, is not what ultimately matters—the overall benefits of the loan are. There are factors that are more important than rate. Factors that, combined with an excellent rate, make for a life-changing, value-based, outstanding loan.

The Truth about the 2 Percent Rule

Perhaps you've heard a reference to the 2 percent rule. Simply stated, this advice argues that you should never refinance unless you can reduce your existing interest rate by at least 2 percent. Although there is validity to this statement, and you certainly can improve your situation dramatically by doing this *right* (which I will cover in detail throughout the book), there are situations where you could reduce your rate by a full 2 percent and actually put yourself in worse shape than you currently are. By the same token, there are other occasions when you can actually increase your rate and still improve your situation greatly. It's all in how you refinance your mortgage.

For example, let's look at a family with an existing 7.0 percent loan and compare it to a proposed 5.0 percent loan. You will see that the 5.0 percent loan is actually worse for the borrower! Afterward, I will show you how a 7.5 percent loan is actually better than both of them! We will be using the Jacksons as an example.

Mr. and Mrs. Jackson have been in their home for five years. They have a balance of $200,000 on their current mortgage loan. The original loan was for $212,500 at a term of thirty years with a fixed interest rate of 7.0 percent. Their current monthly payments, not including taxes and insurance, are $1,413.77.

They have decided to refinance their loan with the sole intention of reducing their monthly payment with no additional cash. They are approved for a thirty-year mortgage for $202,000 at a new fixed interest rate of 5.0 percent; they are financing $2,000 in closing costs (1 percent of the loan amount) in their new loan. The only out-of-pocket cost is an application fee of $300. Based on this, their new monthly payment is going to be $1,084.38, reducing their monthly payment by $329.39.

Let me ask you a few questions:

Did they get a great rate on their loan?

Were the closing costs fair for the loan size?

How much did they save?

Was this a good loan for them?

Your answers are most likely a resounding yes, yes, $329.39, and YES! Believe it or not, the *correct* answers are yes, yes, *nothing*, and NO! Several factors affected and altered their savings. Let me show you the first of these—*the term impact.*

It is true that the Jacksons *will* save $329.39 per month *initially* in comparison to their current mortgage payment, *but for how long?* The answer is only twenty-five years. Why? They already have a thirty-year loan that they have paid on for five years; therefore, they only have twenty-five years remaining. As a result, *they will be extending their loan term by five additional years.* Let's do some simple math to see what they saved and what they lost:

Savings: Twenty-five years (300 months) x $329.39
   monthly savings = $98,817
Loss: Five additional years (60 months) x $1,084.38 new
   payment = $65,063
Net savings: $98,817 savings—$65,063 loss = $33,754
Net monthly savings: $33,754 net savings ÷ 360 months
   (new term) = $93.76

After considering the additional sixty months of payments by extending the Jacksons' term, the actual monthly savings for the new thirty-year term decreased from $329.39 to $93.76! As you can see, the savings was dramatically reduced.

You might be thinking, *But you said they saved NOTHING! It looks to me like they saved almost $100 per month. That's still a lot of money!* You are right, but there are more factors that we are going to look at that will wipe out the $100 it *appears* they are saving. I will get to that after looking at one more vital component of the term impact: the age impact.

The Jacksons are both forty. At this point, they plan to live in their home the rest of their lives. With their current mortgage they would have paid it off at the age of sixty-five, their targeted retirement ages. By extending their term by five years, they pushed their plans to retire with a free and clear home five more years away!

In their current mortgage, when their company retirement pensions would kick in and their work incomes would disappear, they would have still been able to afford retirement because they would have had no mortgage payment. With their new loan, however, they now will either have to continue making mortgage payments for the first five years of retirement or push off retirement for five years until they can afford it. This has both a profound *financial* and *lifestyle* impact.

This leads to a key goal for every mortgage shopper:

◇◇◇

Our goal should always be to get the shortest possible term we can afford to help us get out of debt and prepare for retirement as quickly as possible. By the same token, we should never extend our term on a mortgage refinance.

◇◇◇

Now let's look at another major factor that wipes out the payment savings—*the tax impact*. In addition to extending their term, the Jacksons increased their taxes at the same time. How? The Jacksons currently have a mortgage balance of $200,000 at an annual fixed interest rate of 7.0 percent. That means they will pay approximately $14,000 in mortgage interest this year. We figure this by simply multiplying their mortgage balance ($200,000) by their interest rate (7.0 percent).

In the Jacksons' case, this $14,000 in interest is currently completely tax deductible (I will cover tax deductibility in detail in chapters 3 and 7). Therefore, at the end of the year, they will be able to use this tax deduction to reduce their gross income by

$14,000, saving the tax they would have otherwise paid on that income. The Jacksons are in a 28 percent tax bracket. Therefore, by multiplying the $14,000 mortgage interest deduction by their 28 percent tax bracket, the Jacksons would have saved $3,920 in taxes with their current mortgage.

With their new mortgage they will have a $202,000 balance at a new fixed interest rate of 5.0 percent. By using the same calculation, their mortgage interest reduces to $10,100. That is a cut in their mortgage interest deduction of $3,900. By multiplying this reduction by their 28 percent tax bracket, they lose $1,092 in tax savings at the end of the year. So what did they *actually* save?

The net monthly savings, after extending their term, was $93.76 or $1,125 per year.

However, the Jacksons paid $1,092 in additional taxes because of the decrease in their deductions. They also paid a $300 application fee up front. Combined, their actual cost was $1,392.

Therefore, they saved NOTHING!

At this point you may be thinking, *What if they did not stay thirty years? I don't plan to stay in my house for that long. So if I was in their situation and sold my home or refinanced my mortgage sooner, this would no longer apply to me. I would be saving the full $329.39.* There are two reasons this is wrong— the tax impact, which still applies, and *the principal reduction impact.*

Let's assume for a moment that the Jacksons decided to either sell their home or refinance three years down the road. What would happen? Remember, they originally borrowed $212,500 and have been paying on their current mortgage for five years.

Their balance is $200,000 today. Therefore, after sixty payments, they have reduced their balance by $12,500. In the next three years, they would reduce their balance by another $9,831, taking it down to $190,169.

By refinancing into the 5.0 percent loan, in three years their balance will be $192,594. This is $2,425 more than it would have been had they not refinanced. This will ultimately come out of their proceeds at the closing three years down the road. Divided by the three-year period, that is a loss of $67.36 monthly. This brings the initial $329.39 monthly savings down to $262.03.

You might be thinking, *But they are still saving over $250.* Again, they are not, because of the tax impact. With the reduced principal, the Jacksons will lose $11,405 in mortgage interest tax deductions for that same three years. This results in $3,193 in lost tax savings ($11,405 x 28 percent tax bracket), or $88.70 per month. When you add back the monthly impact of the taxes, the net savings is now around $173 per month. Granted, this is better than nothing, but it is only around half of the original savings. There is still one more problem. If they sell at the end of the three years, they most likely will pay a commission on the sale and closing costs for the house. And if they refinance, they will pay additional loan fees on the new loan and increase their balance again. In either case, they virtually wipe out any savings they created.

In case you are wondering if there is ever a point that the balance would be lower with the 5 percent loan than with the 7 percent loan, the answer is no. If you compared the two loans (by using a loan amortization schedule which compares the interest paid and remaining principal balance for every year of the loan), at no time during the twenty-five years remaining on the 7 percent loan is the balance higher than the same twenty-five years for the 5 percent loan. The gap actually widens each year because even though the interest rate is lower on the 5 percent loan, the Jacksons are five years ahead in payments with the 7 percent loan.

The moral of the story is simply this:

◇◇◇

Rate, in and of itself, is not the primary factor of a great mortgage loan. Rate, combined with the right term, tax savings, and other key factors, make for a great loan!

◇◇◇

To determine the *exact* savings, it is a bit more complex than this. I will break it down in much greater detail in the next chapter to help you better understand it. But you can plainly see from this example that *what you see is not always what you get in mortgage financing.*

So in this scenario, did the lower rate really matter? No, not the way the Jacksons configured the loan. The lower rate would have improved their situation only if they had gotten the 5 percent loan at a twenty-five-year term and did some other things (that I will teach you next) to improve their loan.

One more thing. At the beginning of this section I noted that a 7.5 percent loan was better than both the Jacksons' existing 7.0 percent loan and the proposed 5.0 percent refinance. Here's how. The Jacksons have $25,000 in consumer debt with a payment of $625. Therefore, their *total* debt payments are $2,038.77. If they refinanced their total debt into one loan of $237,350 (includes 1 percent in fees), their total payment would be $1,754, for a twenty-five-year term. Without increasing the term, the payments would reduce $284.77 and give the

Jacksons $10,000 cash at closing. In addition, at 7.5 percent interest their mortgage interest would increase by $7,655 the first year, resulting in $2,143 in additional tax savings based on their tax bracket and a 100 percent interest deduction. This is equivalent to another $178.58 per month in savings.

Therefore, the 7.5 percent saves hundreds of dollars in monthly payments *while* providing $10,000 in cash and thousands in tax savings without extending the term. This clearly provides much greater benefit than either the Jacksons' current 7 percent loan or the 5 percent refinance they have been offered! I will show you many more examples of similar potential savings throughout the rest of this book.

CHAPTER THREE

TAX AND TERM: UNDERSTANDING THE
True Cost

In chapter 2 we determined that the annual percentage rate is more important than the interest rate—although neither are the most important consideration! In fact, APRs and interest rates pale next to the short- and long-term value and savings of *tax and term*. The impact of mortgage tax deductions and the duration of the loan are two of the most critical aspects of mortgage financing.

Tax and *term*—the two Ts of mortgage financing—help us better understand mortgage costs. Let's revisit the scenario of the Jacksons used in the previous chapter, to explain the impact of the two Ts in greater detail. As we go deeper to figure the effect term and taxes have on a mortgage loan, this education can empower you in your next mortgage transaction. Although some analytical formulas in the chapter may seem a little confusing at first, reading through them slowly will help you grasp them. By doing so, it will make the difference for you in either saving or losing tens of thousands of dollars on your next mortgage transaction. Follow along with me as we go through the basic steps to determining and optimizing the tax and term impact.

Clearing the Confusion Surrounding Tax Benefits

One day I was having lunch with my dad, George—a guy with big hands and an even bigger heart. When the check came, I insisted that I pay and told him I could "write it off" on my taxes as a business expense. Instead of trying to wrestle me for the check, as he usually does, he actually let me pay. When I asked why he was letting me pick up the bill so easily, he said that he was doing so "because it isn't costing you anything anyway." His understanding was that I was able to deduct 100 percent of the lunch and therefore it "cost me nothing." It would be great if it really worked that way, but it doesn't.

I still paid $20.00 for lunch out of my pocket. Of course, I could not (and would not) be able to write it off on my taxes. But if it had been tax deductible, I would have received back $7.84 in taxes after filing my income tax return—yet it still would have cost me $12.62 in cash out of my pocket!

◇◇◇

What ultimately matters to you and me in any monetary transaction is the effect on our pocketbook.

◇◇◇

My dad's understanding of taxes was not unlike that of most of us. We have a basic understanding of how taxes work, but not a complete understanding of the implications. As the old saying goes, "We know just enough to be dangerous." In this chapter, you will learn enough about tax, as it pertains to a mortgage loan, to be knowledgeable and confident. I recognize that concepts surrounding taxes—*tax savings*, *benefits*, *liabilities*, and, of course, *calculations*—sometimes can make us feel overwhelmed. Yet all these terms are practical elements of mortgage financing, worth our time. It's worth our time because . . .

◇◇◇

One of the primary benefits to homeownership and mortgage financing is the tax savings.

◇◇◇

As homeowners, if we do not take advantage of the tax benefits associated with mortgage financing, we could actually be better off renting. Therefore, it is important to understand how tax deductibility works to optimize our savings.

Mortgage Interest Is Tax Deductible in Most Cases

It is important to first understand that the interest on mortgage loans, *in most cases*,[1] is tax deductible. This includes first mortgage loans, second mortgage loans, and home equity lines of credit (HELOC). This is a substantial benefit of mortgage financing, particularly when you consider that interest on consumer debt, except student and business loans, has absolutely no tax deductibility. (The government phased out tax deductibility on consumer debt in 1986.)

Understanding the tax benefits to your mortgage loan is of substantial importance to you, as a borrower, in understanding the *true benefits* and *actual cost* of your mortgage loan. Why? Because the tax benefits can change two critical aspects of your loan:

1. the net amount of interest you pay annually, and
2. the actual interest rate after taxes.

The Interest Rate You See Is Almost Never What You Get!

We discussed in chapter 2 the difference between interest rates and APRs. But did you realize that the interest rate you agree to on your loan documents and the actual interest rate you pay after tax are different also? How so? Because of the tax impact a mortgage has on the interest rate. You see, there are two kinds of interest rates: pre-tax and after-tax. Let me define these:

1. The pre-tax interest rate is the rate you pay on your loan *before* the tax benefit.
2. The after-tax interest rate is the rate you pay *after* the tax benefits.

The interest rate, or APR, you see on your loan documents (as discussed in chapter 2) is a pre-tax interest rate. It is the interest rate you pay *before* the tax deduction benefits you receive for mortgage interest. The actual rate you pay *after tax*, depending on the amount of interest you can deduct, is significantly less than what you see on your loan documents. Your loan documents do not reflect this, and in most cases your loan officer will not explain it either (they may not be aware of the difference themselves). Here is an example of a comparison between a pre-tax and after-tax rate:

You borrow $100,000 on a mortgage loan at an annual interest rate of 6 percent before taxes. This is your *pre-tax interest rate.* By multiplying the loan amount by the interest rate you get the *approximate* amount of interest you will pay in the first year. (The actual is a little less because interest decreases each month.) Thus, your approximate annual interest would be $6,000: $100,000 loan amount x 6% = $6,000.

Provided the entire loan balance meets the IRS guidelines for tax deductibility, 100 percent of the interest would be tax deductible. Therefore, in this scenario, you would get a $6,000 *mortgage interest tax deduction.*

Let's calculate your savings in federal taxes. Your federal tax bracket is based on your annual gross income after deductions ("adjusted gross income") as determined by the IRS. (You can view current tax brackets on the IRS Web site at www.irs.gov.) This is important for you to know, as it helps determine how much actual tax savings you will receive from your deduction. To determine your actual tax savings, simply multiply your mortgage interest deduction by your tax bracket. We'll use a 30 percent tax bracket as an example: $6,000 mortgage interest deduction x 30% tax bracket = $1,800 tax savings.

So if you're in the 30 percent tax bracket, you end up paying $1,800 less in federal taxes at the end of the year. This either reduces the amount of tax you owe or increases the amount of your tax refund. Either way, it is *cash to you.* This is where, as a mortgage borrower, tax benefits really affect your pocketbook.

Now, to determine the impact of the tax benefit on your interest rate, let's take this one step further. You paid $6,000 in *pre-tax interest* and received back $1,800 in the form of *tax savings.* Therefore, the *after-tax interest* you paid was only $4,200.

By dividing your *after-tax interest* paid ($4,200) by the loan amount ($100,000), the actual *after-tax interest rate* becomes 4.2 percent in the first year. In other words, your *pre-tax* rate of 6 percent was reduced to an *after-tax* rate of 4.2 percent—a 1.8 percent reduction! The calculation looks like this:

$4,200 after-tax interest paid ÷ $100,000 loan amount = 4.2% after-tax interest rate

◇◇◇

The tax deduction benefits of mortgage interest can significantly reduce both the amount and rate of interest you pay after federal (IRS) tax.

◇◇◇

Clearly, knowing whether you qualify for tax deductibility on your mortgage or home equity loan(s) is important. If you do qualify, determining the exact amount of interest you qualify for will give a better picture of the overall benefits to your mortgage loan. And because the tax benefits change the actual cost of the loan to you annually, this ultimately affects how much you are saving (or losing). This also affects how much you should be borrowing, the purposes for the money, and how you should configure your mortgage loan to gain the greatest tax benefits possible.[2]

In addition, this has a profound impact in a no-cash rate and term refinance, that is, a mortgage where you are refinancing the loan to a lower rate with no additional cash. In a no-cash rate and term refinance you can actually end up paying more taxes instead of less!

The Good, the Bad, and the Ugly of Tax Benefits

Tax deductibility can be one of the most beneficial attributes of a mortgage loan, when approached properly. But it can actually work against you when not approached properly! Millions have *reduced their tax deductions* and *increased their taxes* through mortgage refinancing—all in the name of rate and payment reduction!

Let's look at the Jacksons' scenario again, but this time using *exact* numbers and calculations to both prove this point and help you better understand how to calculate the tax impact:

Mr. and Mrs. Jackson's exact mortgage balance is $200,029 on their current mortgage. Recall that they borrowed $212,500 five years ago at a fixed annual percentage rate of 7.0 percent for a thirty-year term. Their current monthly principal and interest payment is $1,413.77. (You will learn how to figure mortgage payments later.) Mr. and Mrs. Jackson's mortgage qualifies for full tax deductibility with the IRS guidelines; therefore, they can deduct 100 percent of their mortgage interest paid each year. Mr. and Mrs. Jackson are in a 28 percent tax bracket.

Let's look at the estimated mortgage interest deduction they will get over the next twelve months (assuming 100 percent tax deductibility):

$200,029 balance @ 7% interest rate = $13,905.13* actual mortgage interest deduction

*This is the actual amount of mortgage interest the Jacksons will pay in year six based on a loan amortization table for their original $212,500 mortgage loan. This is based on a rate of 7.0% for thirty years

Mr. and Mrs. Jackson are approved for a $202,000 loan for thirty years at a 5.0 percent interest rate. This new loan amount includes the current mortgage balance plus $1,971 in closing costs. Their new payment will be $1,084.38, reducing their current monthly payments by $329.39:

	Loan Balance	Interest Rate	Monthly Payment
Current mortgage	$200,029	7.0%	$1,413.77
New mortgage	$202,000	5.0%	$1,084.38
Monthly payment reduction			$329.39

As we determined in the previous chapter, although Mr. and Mrs. Jackson *are* saving $329.39 before taxes, they will give a portion of it back *after taxes*. Why? Because by reducing their interest rate they also reduced their mortgage interest, which in turn reduces their tax deductions. Let's look at the actual tax impact by comparing the mortgage interest that would have been paid in the sixth year of the current mortgage to the mortgage interest that will be paid in the first year of the new mortgage:

	Balance	Interest Rate	Estimated Loan Mortgage Interest
Current mortgage	$200,029	7.0%	$13,905
New mortgage	$202,000	5.0%	$10,032
Mortgage interest reduction			$3,873

By *reducing their interest rate* from 7 percent to 5 percent, the Jacksons also *reduced their mortgage interest* from $13,905 to $10,032 over the next twelve months. Based on the interest being 100 percent tax deductible, this led to an overall *decrease in their tax deductions* of $3,873 in the coming year. Unfortunately, this will result in a significant decrease in their *after-tax* savings. By multiplying the interest reduction by their 28 percent tax bracket, we see the overall *tax impact* during the first year in increased federal taxes: $3,873 x 28% = $1,084.

Although the Jacksons *decreased* their monthly payment by $329.39 before taxes, they simultaneously *increased* their annual taxes by $1,084. If we take one more step and convert the *annual tax impact* to a *monthly amount* ($1,084 ÷ 12), the monthly payment savings is reduced by $90.33. This changes the after-tax payment savings to $239.06:

Pre-tax Monthly Payment Reduction−	1st Year Monthly Tax Impact =	Adjusted After-tax 1st Year Monthly Payment Reduction
$329.39	$90.33	$239.06

This represents the first-year tax impact only. Although each additional year the mortgage loan is open the tax impact becomes less, it has a critical impact on the overall savings. Therefore, it is a very important consideration in determining the overall cost and value of your mortgage loan! But there is still one other critical consideration that reduces the savings even more—*the term impact.* I will cover both the long-term tax impact and the term impact in the next section.

As you can see, the tax deductions gained from a mortgage loan have a profound impact on the benefits. The idea is to get a mortgage loan that benefits you in every way.

Term: The "Big Kahuna" in Mortgage Financing

Now let's look closer at the term impact. The term (duration) of a loan plays a greater role than any other characteristic in determining the overall cost and value of a mortgage transaction. Let me prove this by looking closer at the Jacksons' situation again. I will be rounding numbers to the nearest dollar to make things simple.

Mr. and Mrs. Jackson have a thirty-year term on their current mortgage. They have twenty-five years remaining. With the new loan they are considering at 5.0 percent, their payment would reduce by $329 before taxes and $239 after taxes in the first year. But the payment reduction *is not* for thirty years, only for the twenty-five years *remaining*. If we multiply the pre-tax payment reduction of $329 (we will leave out the tax impact for now to make this easier) by the twenty-five years (300 payments), the *total payment savings for the twenty-five-year period* becomes $98,817.

This total payment savings is not the *actual* savings, as it is *offset* by the five years the Jacksons extended their term. By multiplying their new payment ($1,084.38) by this sixty-month extension, we see a cost of $65,063 in additional payments:

Current Remaining Term –	New Term =	Difference x	New Monthly Payment =	Term Impact
25 years	30 years	5 years (60 months)	$1,084.38	$65,063

By subtracting the *term impact* of $65,063 from the total payment savings of $98,817, we get a net savings, before taxes, of $33,754 for the new loan. Finally, by dividing this net savings ($33,754) by the new loan term of thirty years (360 months), we see the actual payment savings each month is $94 *after the term impact:* $33,754 ÷ 360 = $94.

Based on the *term impact alone, before the tax impact*, the initial payment reduction of $329 is cut by more than two-thirds! When you factor the tax impact into all of this, it gets even worse.

Term and Tax Impact in the Long Term

Instead of looking at just the first-year impact, as we did

earlier, this time we will look at the term and tax impact over the entire life of the loan. We will do this by comparing the total interest they would have paid for their current 7.0 percent loan to that of the new 5.0 percent loan they are considering.

Recall that the Jacksons took out their original $212,500 loan for thirty years at 7.0 percent. The total interest for the thirty years is $296,456. In the first five years of that loan they have paid $72,355 in interest, leaving $224,101 to be paid off. The new loan for $202,000 at 5 percent will have a total interest of $188,376. The difference is $35,725—this represents the *total interest reduction.* This is why the monthly payments are going down. As you will see, it is also why their taxes are going to go up.

Because the Jacksons' mortgage interest was 100 percent tax deductible, this $35,725 represents the difference in the mortgage interest deductions. By multiplying this $35,725 by the Jacksons' 28 percent tax bracket, we see the actual *tax impact* to their income: $35,725 x 28% = $10,003. *They will lose $10,003 in tax savings over the remaining term of their loan.*

To see the impact to the monthly savings, we simply divide the tax impact ($10,003) by the new thirty-year loan (360 months). This gives us a clear picture of the *net monthly tax impact* for this loan. This amount will reduce their original payment savings: $10,003 ÷ 360 = $28. The Jacksons will lose $28 in monthly tax savings.

Now let's subtract both the tax and term impact to see the actual savings for the new loan. The total payment savings for the twenty-five years was $98,817 (300 months x $329.39). The five-year extension cost the Jacksons $65,063 in term impact and the loss in mortgage interest deductions cost them another

$10,003. If we subtract these from the original savings, the net savings is $23,751:

Total Payment Savings (Remaining Term) −	Term Impact −	Tax Impact =	Net Total Savings after Term and Tax Impact
$98,817	$65,063	$10,003	$23,751

Finally, to break this down to the simplest component—monthly savings—we divide the net savings ($23,751) by the new thirty-year term: $23,751 ÷ 360 = $66.00.

Here is the bottom line: The original $329.39 monthly payment savings that the Jacksons thought they were getting was reduced to $66 *after the tax and term impact!* In other words, the Jacksons gave back 80 percent of their original savings in the form of taxes and term—a significant reduction. If you are thinking that is still better than nothing, remember that they gave back five years of their life and retirement, also. With their current mortgage, they would have been sixty-seven when their home was paid off: their targeted retirement age. But with their new mortgage they will now be seventy-two. It is hard to put a price on the cost of those five years from both a financial and lifestyle perspective.

Term and Tax Impact in the Short Term

Let's look at one more scenario. What would have happened to the Jacksons if they had taken the new loan and then sold or refinanced three years later?

Had the Jacksons decided to refinance their current 7 percent mortgage loan to the 5 percent new mortgage, at the end of three years they would have paid down $9,406 on their principal, resulting in a mortgage balance of $192,594. Had they kept their current mortgage, however, their principal mortgage balance at the end of that same period would have been $190,170. Therefore, if after three years they decided to sell and purchase a new home or refinance again, their balance would have been $2,424 higher with the lower interest rate loan. The end result is less cash at closing in the case of a home sale, or a higher balance to pay off in the case of a refinance. In either event, it is a $2,424 cost to the Jacksons. Divided by the three-year period, that is a cost of $67 monthly:

Current Mortgage Balance –	New Mortgage Balance =	Principal Reduction Impact ÷	Term =	Monthly Short-term Impact
$190,170	$192,594	($2,424)	36 Months	($67)

If you subtract this monthly payment impact ($67) from the initial payment reduction ($329), the *net payment reduction before taxes* drops to $262.

Let's look at the tax impact again. With their original 7.0 percent mortgage loan, the Jacksons would have paid $41,036 in mortgage interest for the three-year period. In that same three years, they would pay $29,632 with their 5.0 percent mortgage loan. The result is a reduction of $11,404 in mortgage interest for that three-year period:

3 Year Mortgage Interest Paid (Current 7% Loan) –	3 Year Mortgage Interest Paid (New 5% Loan) =	Mortgage Interest Reduction
$41,036	$29,632	$11,404

By multiplying their 28 percent tax bracket by their mortgage interest reduction of $11,404, we see that the Jacksons have a greater tax burden—$3,193 in higher federal taxes.

By dividing this tax increase of $3,193 by the three-year (thirty-six month) period, they discover they will pay $89 more in taxes each month. Therefore, we can see that the net savings *after term and tax* is only $173 by simply subtracting the monthly short-term impact ($67) and the monthly tax impact ($89) from the initial payment reduction ($329):

Monthly Payment Reduction before Term and Tax −	Monthly Short-term Impact −	Monthly Tax Impact =	Net Monthly Payment Reduction
$329	$67	$89	$173

At $173 per month, the net savings is about half the original payment savings. If the Jacksons end up selling, they will most likely pay a commission on the sale and closing costs that will wipe out any savings. If they end up refinancing, they will most likely pay additional loan fees on the new loan, increase their balance, and maybe even stretch the term again. It becomes a never ending cycle of debt that eats up the Jacksons' financial future!

Clearly, this is not the best approach. Throughout the remainder of this book, I will offer guidelines for purchasing or refinancing a home with a mortgage loan and optimizing the monetary benefits a mortgage loan and your home's equity can bring. Along the way, you will be equipped to negotiate and consummate every future mortgage loan so that you get the best rate, at the best loan amount, for the best payment, at the best term to suit your personal financial situation, both short- and long-term.

We will begin by looking at the monetary benefits of having a mortgage loan.

NOTES

1. Although every mortgage loan has some level of tax deductibility, each year every loan has to meet a set of guidelines established by the Internal Revenue Service (IRS) that determine the amount of tax deductibility for that loan. A good portion, if not all, of the interest you pay on most mortgage loans has a tax benefit. The amounts and requirements regarding what is allowable to deduct in a mortgage loan by the IRS changes annually. It is imperative that you consult a tax advisor or refer to the current IRS guidelines whenever entering into a mortgage transaction to understand what portion of your mortgage loan qualifies for tax deduction benefits.

2. As a reminder, the APR guidelines established by the federal government do not reflect the after-tax interest rate, only the pre-tax interest rate, because not every mortgage loan qualifies for 100 percent tax deductibility. The criteria changes annually, and also depends on the borrower's personal situation and the purposes for the loan. It is important that you seek a professional tax advisor to determine how much of your mortgage loan is tax deductible before finalizing any mortgage transaction. The reason I recommend a certified professional tax advisor is that they understand the highly technical regulations and what is allowable. By doing it on your own, this could be a very overwhelming and confusing process that could lead to costly mistakes.

CHAPTER FOUR

YOUR MORTGAGE AS AN INVESTMENT
Tool

There is much more to the value of a mortgage than just the interest rate and fees (or price). The *true value* is defined not by the price, but by the benefits you get. You may recall that "price is what you pay and value is what you get, and it's not what you pay that matters, but it's what you get." In a mortgage transaction, what you *pay* is the rate, points, and fees (price), and what you *get* is the loan amount (cash), the payment (monthly cost), and the term (payback). Therefore, the true value of any mortgage loan is determined by the benefits created through choosing the right loan amount, the right payment, and the right term.

In the next several chapters, we are going to take everything you have learned thus far and apply it to converting a mortgage loan into a powerful savings and life investment tool. You will discover how to create benefits, both short- and long-term, that will help you achieve your true financial and life goals.

Developing Long-term Life Goals

Because a mortgage transaction is not only the largest but also the longest transaction we typically ever enter into, it is one where we should consider all of our long-term life goals. And because a mortgage is really *money*, it is a transaction that should take into consideration *both* our short- and long-term financial goals.

Our life financial goals must include three key considerations.

First, short-term cash flow objectives (payment). First and foremost, we must determine the monthly payment we can afford. In a mortgage refinance, this is a key determination in how much we need to reduce our payment, what debts we need to pay off, and what terms we are going to choose. In a purchase transaction this directly determines the amount of home we can afford. We never want to enter into a mortgage transaction getting a payment that we cannot manage comfortably.

Second, short- and long-term financial needs (cash). In addition to the payment, we want to establish the amount of cash we need to achieve both our short- and long-term financial goals. We tend to borrow only for what we need today (debt consolidation, home improvement, home purchase, etc.), instead of also thinking for the future. Because our home is usually our greatest resource for accessing cash, we want to enter every mortgage transaction considering both the *immediate* cash needs and *future* financial goals. This includes not just the financing of debt or the purchasing of our home, but cash for important life decisions like our retirement, investments, college funds, and emergency funds.

Third, long-term cost and impact to life goals (term). We tend to look at our mortgage as our largest *debt* instead of as our largest *investment.* The truth is that our mortgage is a major investment and component of our overall financial picture. We need to consider how our mortgage plays into our overall life goals and financial plan, including our long-term retirement plans, debt-free plans, estate plans, and future wealth. This means considering the cost of the loan over the term, the age we will be when the mortgage is paid off, and the tax implications to the mortgage, both short and long term.

These are critical considerations that need to be weighed when we are contemplating our next mortgage transaction. Coincidentally, these considerations tie in directly to the benefits, or value, of the mortgage loan. Having said that, let's take a closer look at the *Four Major Monetary Benefits* for both refinance and purchase transactions that directly affect the monetary value of the loan. The more we improve each of these benefits, the more money we either save or gain in our mortgage loan and the more we make it a true investment tool:

1. The monthly payment
2. The cash or loan amount
3. The tax benefits
4. The term

These monetary benefits represent the four primary benefit *components* of a mortgage loan. Our objective here is simple if we want to get a mortgage that is truly beneficial:

◇◇◇

**Optimize each of the four monetary benefits to
create the greatest loan and overall savings possible for
both today and the future.**

◇◇◇

Let's look at these four monetary benefits from a life-goals perspective.

Primary Monetary Benefit #1: The Monthly Payment

As mentioned earlier, the monthly payment amount is the first consideration we need to make in choosing a mortgage loan, as the payment ultimately impacts both the *amount* and *term* of the loan. The amount of the loan will determine how much cash we get. The term of the loan will determine the ultimate payback, or total payments, for the life of the loan. The payment also determines the subsequent impact to our monthly cash flow (income minus payments). The more we maximize (increase) our payment, the more cash and/or the shorter the term we may be able to get, but the more we reduce our monthly cash flow. Conversely, the more we minimize (decrease) the payment, the less cash and/or the longer term we get and the more monthly cash flow we have available. Our objective is to find the perfect balance between these two. Let's examine the impact payment makes in a refinance and purchase.

Refinance: Our payment choice not only determines the amount of money we may save and the amount of cash we may get in the short term, but also the term we ultimately choose and the long-term costs of the mortgage.

Purchase: Our payment choice not only determines the amount of money we will get and the amount of home we can buy in the short term, but also the term we ultimately choose and the long-term costs of the mortgage.

◇◇◇

To maximize the payment benefit, choose a payment that provides the maximum cash and term benefits while at the same time creating the ideal cash flow for your personal situation.

◇◇◇

Primary Monetary Benefit #2: The Cash or Loan Amount

The second consideration is the amount of cash we access through a mortgage loan. This is achieved through determining the right loan amount to meet our cash needs.

Refinance: By maximizing the equity in our home we in turn optimize the amount of cash we can access. By converting our equity into cash we can create powerful cash benefits only under two conditions: the cash is used for *debt elimination* and/or *sound investments.* (Sound investments are defined in chapter 6.)

Purchase: In a purchase transaction, the more we maximize the value in the home by borrowing against it, the less cash we need to put down on the property and the more cash we have to use for sound investments.

◇◇◇

To maximize the cash benefit, borrow the ideal amount of cash that improves your overall financial picture.

◇◇◇

Primary Monetary Benefit #3: The Tax Benefits

The third component to consider is the tax benefits of a mortgage loan. Because mortgage interest is generally tax deductible (as covered in chapter 3), we want to be sure we are borrowing in a way that maximizes the tax benefits available. The amount and purpose(s) of a mortgage, as well as the way we configure the loan, not only determine the benefits, but also the tax implications. (Always consult your tax advisor to determine the actual tax savings for your loan before completing the transaction.)

Refinance: In a cash-out refinance, by paying off personal debt or accessing additional cash, we can increase our tax deductions and gain substantial tax benefits. In a rate and term refinance, we can actually decrease our tax deductions. In addition, when using cash for investment purposes, there are tax ramifications that can lead to tax benefits or liabilities, depending on the type of investments we choose. In either case, we need to understand both the short- and long-term tax implications.

Purchase: The larger the loan amount, the greater the tax deductions generally. Therefore, when considering our down payment, we want to take into consideration the advantages, or disadvantages, of increasing or decreasing the amount based on the tax implications.

◇◇◇

To maximize the tax benefit, borrow in such a way that you maximize your tax savings while minimizing your tax liabilities.

◇◇◇

Primary Monetary Benefit #4: The Term

In addition to, and in conjunction with, the payment and cash and tax benefits, is the importance of choosing the right term. This is the fourth, and possibly most important, consideration. The term directly affects our payment, our payback, and our long-term debt freedom. By maximizing the payment to obtain the shortest possible term we can afford, we pay off the mortgage in the shortest time period possible. This can save us tens, if not hundreds, of thousands of dollars in interest, build up our equity quicker, eliminate our debt faster, and reduce the age we will be at the time of payoff.

Refinance: In a refinance transaction we must first consider the term remaining on the existing mortgage. We never want to offset our short-term benefits of payment, cash, and tax by extending term and increasing the long-term costs of the loan. In addition, we want to build our term around both our short-term cash flow and our long-term debt freedom and retirement objectives to maximize the term benefits.

Purchase: In a purchase transaction, we want to consider the minimum term possible to both reduce the overall payback, or total cost of the loan, as well as build equity faster by increasing our principal reduction. Once again, we want to build our term around both our short-term cash flow and our long-term debt freedom and retirement objectives to maximize the term benefits.

◇◇◇

To maximize the term benefit, choose a term that provides you an affordable payment while maximizing the term reduction and minimizing the payback.

◇◇◇

In the following chapters, we are going to take each one of these four major monetary benefits and go deeper so we can build a strategy for developing a mortgage loan, whether a refinance or purchase, with true intrinsic value. When configured correctly, a mortgage loan can be a life-changing investment. The key word here is *configure*. The loan configuration (which includes the loan amount, use of the cash, term, and payment) dictates either the *true value or actual loss* you create through your mortgage loan.

CHAPTER FIVE

CHOOSING A PAYMENT FOR
True Savings

T he monthly payment. It's the first consideration in choosing a mortgage loan, even before we consider the loan amount. Our goal here is twofold: to get the maximum payment possible that is also the most affordable payment. By maximizing the monthly payment we optimize the cash, tax, term, and deferral benefits (covered later), and by choosing an affordable payment we keep from creating a financial burden.

There is a delicate balance between these two concepts.

One of the biggest mistakes we can make in either refinancing a mortgage or purchasing a home is our payment choice. Typically when we purchase a home, we tend to put ourselves into the biggest payment we can to get the most house for our money. (Remember, 87 percent of all fixed-term mortgages in 2007 were for thirty years or longer.) Then later, when we refinance, we take the exact opposite approach and try to get the lowest payment we can, again at the longest term possible, to reduce our payments by the greatest amount possible.

We Unknowingly Choose the Worst Possible Payment

In other words, we *unknowingly* put ourselves in the worst possible situation when trying to create the best possible situation. *We take on more house at a longer term than we should, only to try to lower the payment and extend the term later!* How many of us have done this? Pretty painful when we think about it!

Remember in chapter 1 when I said that rate is not the number one consideration in a mortgage transaction? The interest rate directly affects the payment, not the term or loan amount. The higher the rate, the higher the payment. But keep in mind this fact:

◇◇◇

Payment generally has far less impact on the total cost of a mortgage than the term does.

◇◇◇

Let me give you an example. Assume we are choosing between two companies both offering us thirty-year mortgage loans for $250,000. Lender A is at 6.0 percent with a payment of $1,498.88 and Lender B is at 6.25 percent with a payment of $1,539.29. The difference in the monthly payments is $40.41. If we look at this from a life-of-loan perspective, or total payback, the difference in the total cost between the two loans is $14,548.68 (360 payments x the $40.41 difference). Obviously, Lender A is the better choice.

Look at the scenario again. Lender A will only offer a thirty-year loan option. Lender B, on the other hand, offers a twenty-five-year loan option. The new payment for Lender B, at the same 6.25 percent for twenty-five years, is $1,649.17. Therefore, the difference is now $150.29. Which is the lower cost loan now? In the short term, it's Lender A, but in the long term, Lender B. Even though the rate and payment are higher, because of the shortened term, the total payback over the life of the loan with Lender B is $44,845.80 less.

So the rate and payment generally have less impact than the term. Yet most of us put more emphasis on the amount of our monthly payments than the length (term) of the payments. Because term is the primary driver to the total payback and the ultimate interest we pay, or cost of the loan, it is a critical aspect of the total value of your mortgage. Remember, price is what you pay and value is what you get. It is not what you pay that ultimately matters, but what you get.

Reverse Your Thinking Today!

To truly get the best payment, we should reverse our thinking. With a purchase, we want to get the *maximum affordable payment at the shortest term*, not the longest, and we should be *very conservative in the amount of home and corresponding size of payment we take on.* This kind of thinking will protect us in the case of future changes to our situation or the market. Think about the mortgage woes of 2007 and 2008. Had people chosen more affordable housing and shorter-term loans, two critical things would have happened:

1. Many would still have been able to afford the homes in the market downturn.
2. They would have decreased their principal balance faster, creating more of an equity cushion to sell the home or refinance to a lower payment.

The options significantly improve when you choose the right payment that leads to the right term and loan amount.

In a mortgage refinance, you want to choose the highest

payment you can comfortably afford to get the shortest term possible. This creates a discipline that will force you to reduce your mortgage balance faster, build equity more quickly, and become debt-free sooner. Let me expand upon the payment benefit for a refinance.

Creating True Payment Benefits in a Refinance Transaction

In an *ideal* mortgage refinance, you can . . .

- reduce your payments *while*
- accessing cash *while*
- reducing your taxes *while*
- reducing your term *while*
- saving money in payments for the thirty-day period after the loan!

This is the kind of refinance that truly makes a life-changing difference. By qualifying for a refinance, it does not mean you will qualify for *all* of these benefits, but you will qualify for some. There are three determining factors that will dictate *how many* and *to what extent* of benefits you will qualify for:

1. The amount of equity you have to work with.
2. The amount of personal debt and payments you can leverage.
3. The amount of income you have to determine what kind of payment you can afford.

The more of these three factors you have, the more benefits you will be able to create for yourself. Ultimately, every circumstance is different, but there may be possibilities to change your life financially far beyond anything you have ever imagined.

Maximizing an Affordable Refinance Payment

The more we maximize our payment in a mortgage refinance, the more benefits we create. The higher the payment, the more cash we can access *and/or* the shorter the term we can achieve.

Remember, there are only three primary components to a loan: the loan amount, the term, and the payment. By increasing or decreasing the payment, we affect either or both of the other two components. By reducing our payment we reduce the loan amount and/or extend the term, and by increasing our payment we increase the loan amount and/or shorten the term.

We always want to maximize the payment in such a way to get the greatest amount of cash available at the shortest possible term. This allows us to optimize our equity and benefits while minimizing our payback and term.

Importance of Payment to a Refinance

The payment you choose in a mortgage refinance directly affects the ultimate benefits you will receive. The payment not only influences the term, but it also determines the loan amount, or total amount of cash you will get. This determines:

1. *How much debt you can pay off.* Because the payment dictates the loan amount, the larger the loan amount, the more cash you will have access to for debt consolidation.
2. *How much payment savings you can create.* The more

debts you have, typically the higher the debt-to-payment relationship. Therefore, the more debts you can pay off, generally the more payment savings you can create. (Caution: accessing cash from your equity can be a detrimental choice unless done under the right circumstances for the right reasons. I will discuss those reasons in chapter 6.)

3. *How much additional cash you can get for life goals.* In addition, the more you increase the payment, the bigger the loan amount you can create and the more cash you get for achieving major short- and long-term financial and life goals.

4. *How much tax deductibility you will receive.* The bigger the loan becomes, generally the more mortgage interest you create and the bigger the tax deduction becomes (always consult your tax advisor to determine the tax benefits and liabilities of your mortgage loan before completing the transaction).

5. *What term you will get and the long-term cost.* The more you increase the payment on your mortgage, the shorter the term you can create. This will have a major impact on the total cost of the loan over the term as well as the amount of principal reduction each year.

6. *How much payment deferral savings you will end up with.* The payment deferral, which will be covered in detail in a later chapter, increases as you pay off more debts.

Again, the common mistake we make in a mortgage refinance is searching for the lowest possible payment. In doing so, we optimize the payment benefit, but many times minimize the cash, tax, term, and deferral benefits. As a result, we achieve only one of the many monetary benefits available through mortgage refinancing (and usually the least beneficial), and we miss out on a chance to enhance our lives financially. At the same time, we wipe out our short-term savings by creating additional costs in the long term. This is a critical mistake we never want to make again!

◇◇◇

For the best payment benefit in a refinance transaction, choose an affordable payment that maximizes the loan amount while minimizing the payment reduction benefit, so you can optimize the other benefits (cash, tax, term, and deferral).

◇◇◇

Eliminating "Debt-trimental" Burdens

You may have noticed the first area to consider in a mortgage refinance is "how much debt you can pay off." Did you know that you can actually use your personal debt to eliminate your total debt? It is true—your debt can actually be the key to becoming debt free! A refinance not only can improve your payment, taxes, and term, it can also help you pay off personal debts. Our goal should always be to get out of debt as quickly as we possibly can. Personal debt can lead to serious issues with our health, our well-being, our relationships, and our sanity! All debt must go! Bottom line: it is simply "debt-trimental"!

The Bible gives us great instruction on debt in Romans 13:8: "Owe nothing to anyone—except for your obligation to love one another." To do this, we must begin by first looking at how to *analyze and understand* our debt so we can determine our *options* for eliminating it and then develop a *plan* for execution. This all begins by determining one of the most important and revolutionary concepts you will learn in this book: *debt-to-payment relationship*, or "DPR."

Consider this simple truth—*all debt is debt.* As I mentioned in chapter 1, we tend to compartmentalize our debt between personal debt and mortgage debt. The reality is all debt is an encumbrance in our lives; it is money that is owed and must be repaid with interest. Any debt can result in a lien on our house if we do not pay it. *Debt is dangerous!*

Know Your Debt and Payments (Liabilities)

When was the last time you sat down and added up *every debt* you have and *every payment* you owe? When was the last time you compared those debts and payments to *every asset* you own and *every dollar* you make? For most of us, we go through life, month after month, simply paying the bills as they come in and hoping there is money left at the end. This is no way to manage your debt. We must take a *proactive* approach.

The very first step to financial freedom and debt elimination is to completely understand your debt. This means knowing the *who, what, when,* and *how* of your debt: who you owe, what you owe, when it will be paid off, and how you will accomplish that. Start by analyzing and totaling every debt and payment you have to determine your *total liabilities.* This is essential to debt elimination and wealth management.

Understand and Determine Your DPR Opportunities

Once you have determined your liabilities, the next step is to determine your debt-to-payment relationship (DPR), or your *opportunities.* Debt elimination begins with understanding this concept. So what is a DPR? It is the relationship between what you pay and what you owe. *DPR is the clearest indicator available of the disproportion between your debt and payments and the opportunity to reduce and ultimately eliminate them!*

DPR is the key to both understanding your liabilities and determining your opportunities. Here's just one example. Harry and Helen Hunter are paying $2,002 a month on their thirty-year mortgage, two cars, two bank credit cards, and two department store credit cards. (Like millions today, the Hunters are suffering under the burden of installment and credit card debt, with interest rates up to 23 percent. The fact is that even the low-rate credit card is not fixed and is subject to increasing in multiple ways. In addition, if the Hunters ever run past their due date there is a likelihood they will be charged an added $29 to $39 late fee. There are many reasons that credit card debt is the most "debt-trimental" of all debts. You can learn more about "The Simple Truth about Credit Card Debt" at our Web site at www.mortgagempowered.com.) Let's determine their DPR.

Determining the Debt-to-Payment Relationship

Debt	Original Amount	Interest Rate	Current Principal Balance	Payment
Mortgage	$150,000	6.0%	$144,126	$899
Car loan	$25,000	5.5%	$20,533	$477
Car loan	$17,000	6.0%	$10,803	$328
MC	$7,500	7.0%	$5,318	$133
Visa	$5,000	13.25%	$3,247	$81
Dept. store	$1,500	23%	$875	$35
Dept. store	$1,500	23%	$1,214	$49
Debt-to Payment Relationship (DPR)			$186,116	$2,002

The Hunters' total debts are $186,116 with total payments of $2,002. These two numbers represent their DPR. By looking at their DPR, we can easily determine if their payments are too high in comparison to the debt. How do we do that? Initially, by applying the 1 percent rule, which examines your debt-to-payment relationship. The 1 percent rule says: Multiply your balances times 1 percent and if your payments are more than the resulting amounts, you are paying too much. But there is an even more accurate way to know *exactly* how much too much you are paying . . .

It's EPIC!

By applying the 1 percent rule to the Hunters' situation, we find that the $186,116 debt yields a payment of $1,861. This *immediately* tells us their payments are most likely too high. But to really understand how high and confirm they are *really* paying too much, we apply the *equal payment investment calculation (EPIC)*. To figure EPIC, calculate the current debt balances as a loan amount at the current prevailing mortgage rates for a payment equal to the current total payments to determine the new term. This is a calculation that indeed can have *epic* ramifications to their debt!

For example, the remaining term on the Hunters' current mortgage was twenty-seven years. If we take the total monthly payment of $2,002 and calculate it at a 6.5 percent rate (closer to typical prevailing mortgage interest rates) for the *total debt* of $186,116, their term to pay off the new loan would be ten years, ten months. In other words, *by paying the same payment on one loan that combines all of the different debts, they would be debt free in 10.8 years.* That is a reduction of 16.2 years (60 percent), or 194.4 months, from the current mortgage term.

One more tip. If your monthly gross income—all income before taxes—divided by your total debt payments (mortgage loan, car loans, bank and other credit card payments) is more than 30 percent, you are definitely in need of debt and payment reduction. This percentage is known as the debt-to-income ratio, or DTI.[1] (We cover this and how to qualify for a mortgage finance in much greater detail in chapters 9 and 10.)

Drop the Payback Period—and Save on Interest!

You may be thinking, *By rolling my debt into the mortgage loan, I would be extending the term on the cars and credit cards.* The answer is yes and no. As you can see in the following chart, the term for the Hunters' personal (non-mortgage) debt, which represents only 14 percent of that total debt, increases; but by including (or leveraging) the monthly payments for these debts as part of the mortgage refinance, the number of years on the mortgage actually decreased— significantly. As a result, the total payback for all of the debt dropped dramatically. Because all of these debts are currently open-ended terms, the remaining terms were determined by calculating the current balances at the current payments based on the current interest rates for each of the debts. These terms are not actual, as they assume no increase in the balance (credit use) and no change in the payments or interest rates for the remaining terms. Actual terms would likely be much longer, increasing the ultimate term reduction and the corresponding savings for the debts.

Debt (Remain. Term)	Current Payment	Total of Current Payments	New Term Reduction/ Increase	Portion of New Pmt.*	Total of New Pmts.	Savings or Increase
Mortg. (27 yrs)	$899	$291,276	(16.2 Yrs)	$1,551	$201,009	($90,267)
Car loan (4 yrs)*	$477	$22.896	+ 6.8 Yrs	$221	$28,641	$5,745
Car loan (3 yrs)*	$328	$11,808	+ 7.8 Yrs	$116	$15,033	$3,225
MasterCard (3.8 yrs)*	$133	$6,065	+7 Yrs	$57	$7.387	$1,322
Visa (4.5 yrs)*	$81	$4,374	+ 6.3 Yrs	$35	$4,536	$162
Store (2.9 yrs)*	$35	$1,218	+ 7.9 Yrs	$9	$1,166	($52)
Store (2.8 yrs)*	$49	$1,646	+ 8 Yrs	$13	$1,684	$38
Totals	$2,002	$339,283		$2,002	$259,456	($79,827)

*Determined by calculating the amount of each individual debt (excluding the mortgage loan) at the new term of 10.8 years for the interest rate of 6.50 percent. This shows the actual monthly cost of each debt as a portion of the total monthly payment of $2,002.

Because of the significant reduction in the term of the mortgage, which represents 86 percent of the Hunters' debt, there is a substantial savings in loan interest. Although we extended the terms on the personal debt, and the total increase to the amount the Hunters pay back on that portion of the debt is $10,440, by decreasing the term on the mortgage, the total payback on the mortgage decreases $90,267. The net result is a substantial savings in total payments and payback—nearly $80,000—without changing their current payments one penny! In addition, they are free from *all* debt in 10.8 years. (This assumes no increase in credit card balances nor in the payments nor interest rates for the remaining terms, which is unlikely.)[2] Assuming they are age forty-five (an average refinance age), the age at payoff of the mortgage would change to fifty-six instead of seventy-two! So the Hunters save not just years, but dollars.

Lastly, remember that we used assumptions for the credit card debts that the balances, payments, and interest rates did not change. In actuality, these would most likely change, resulting in even longer terms and greater savings through refinancing. In addition, none of the Hunters' personal debts are tax deductible in their current non-mortgage state. By converting them into mortgage debt, there is a possibility that the interest will become tax deductible. If so, the personal debts, which represented $41,990 of the Hunters' total debt, would result in $16,554 in total interest paid over the new term. If 100 percent of the interest qualified for a mortgage interest tax deduction, at a 28 percent tax bracket they would save an additional $4,635 in taxes over the term of the loan!

Four Fascinating Refinance Scenarios

Let's look at some examples of how reducing the term can affect the payment amounts of a mortgage and cash benefits *with or without debt consolidation.* In all of these scenarios, we will use a 6.5 percent interest rate for our calculations and, for simplicity purposes, will not include any points or fees. Any points or fees paid would simply come out of the total savings created for each scenario. We will address points and fees in later chapters.

Changing the payment, term, and/or cash options of a refinance all can have differing outcomes for elements of the mortgage loan. Using the Hunters' financial numbers as the example, consider refinance scenario #1, where the total monthly debt payment changes from the current $2,002 a month.

Refinance Scenario #1: Payment Impact to Term

As you can see in the chart below, by changing the payment and keeping the loan amount the same, we dramatically change the term.

Reduced Payment and Term Options

Category	Current	Option 1	Option 2	Option 3	Option 4
Debt/loan mortgage amount	$186,116	$186,116	$186,116	$186,116	$186,116
Total payments	$2,002	$1,176	$1,257	$1,387	$1,621
Payment reduction	N/A	$826	$745	$615	$381
Term	27 Years	30 Years	25 Years	20 Years	15 Years
Term difference	N/A	+ 3 Years	(2 Years)	(7 Years)	(12 Years)

Option 1 used a traditional thirty-year loan that most borrowers choose. This is by far the worst option. Although the payment reduction of $826 is the greatest, the current term is extended by three years. This negates the savings.

In option 2, although the Hunters' payment is $81 more, they still achieve a substantial payment reduction of $745 *while* reducing the term by two years. By simply applying $81 of the monthly *savings* they could have had in option 1 to the payment in option 2, they reduce the term by five years! Clearly, the twenty-five-year term is a far better option than the thirty-year term.

But option 3, the twenty-year term, is even better. The payment reduction is still substantial at $615, but the term reduction from the current remaining term is now seven years and ten years less than the thirty-year option. And option 4 provides the greatest term reduction at twelve years, while still reducing the payments by $315! Every option *except* option 1 reduces *both* the payments and the term.

◇◇◇

The fact of the matter is that a thirty-year term refinance almost never makes sense!

◇◇◇

Refinance Scenario #2: Payment Impact to Long-term Payback

Let's look at the Hunters' chart (condensed) again from a payback standpoint. Do the shorter terms truly make sense from the overall payback?

Payback on Reduced Payment and Term Options

Category	Current	Option 1	Option 2	Option 3	Option 4
Debt/loan amount	$186,116	$186,116	$186,116	$186,116	$186,116
Payments	$2,002	$1,176	$1,257	$1,387	$1,621
Term	27 Years	30 Years	25 Years	20 Years	15 Years
Term payback	$339,283	$423,360	$377,100	$332,880	$291,780
Payback difference	N/A	+ $84,077	+ $37,817	($6,403)	($47,503)

Although the monthly payments are drastically reduced in *every case*, the total payback for options 1 and 2 are greater.

However, options 3 and 4 not only reduce the payments and term substantially, but also decrease the total payback. In the case of option 4 there is a total payback reduction of $47,503. If this was your situation, that money could go to savings, retirement, or college funding instead of interest!

Clearly, the more you can maximize the payment and minimize the monthly savings, the better the *overall* benefits become. As you can see in the chart, the payment reduction does not change much until you get to the fifteen-year term.

◇◇◇

The more we can maximize the payment, the shorter the term of the loan. The shorter the term of the loan, the more we save overall, and the sooner we are debt free!

◇◇◇

Having looked at the impact to both term and payback, now let's look at the impact payment can have to the cash we can access through our mortgage loan. In the next scenario, we will simply match the current payment and, by changing the terms, see what it does to the cash value of the loan.

Refinance Scenario #3: Payment Impact to Cash

Now consider what happens if the Hunters were to keep the same payment amount but seek varying cash-out options during the refinancing.

By matching the current payment and applying the same terms as the previous scenarios, the Hunters dramatically change the cash amount. Although the thirty-year option provides the most cash, because it is the longest term option, when you consider the offset of the increased term and long-term costs, it is clearly not the best option for the Hunters—or you. The twenty-five year (option 2) or twenty year (option 3), depending on your cash needs, provide better *total* benefits because both provide substantial cash *and* term reductions at the same time!

Same Payment and Cash-out Options

Category	Current	Option 1	Option 2	Option 3	Option 4
Payments	$2,002	$2,002	$2,002	$2,002	$2,002
Debt/loan amt.	$186,116	$316,738	$296,501	$268,518	$229,822
Term	27 Years	30 Years	25 Years	20 Years	15 Years
Term difference	N/A	+ 3 Years	(2 Years)	(7 Years)	(12 Years)
Additional cash	$0	$130,622	$110,385	$82,402	$43,706

Remember, in every scenario, we simply paid the same payment we were already paying; we did not increase our current payments one cent. But by *leveraging* our debt and payments, and refinancing them into a mortgage loan, we created immediate cash availability. This is like getting money for nothing! (This will be discussed further in chapter 6.)

Refinance Scenario #4: Payment Impact to Term and Cash

Look at one more scenario in which we combine all of these benefits: payment reduction, term reduction, and cash. This time we will leave out the thirty-year option and *only* provide options that improve all three components of the loan: the payment, the cash, and the term. This is where we start to make an impact on every aspect of our financial picture:

Reduced Payment, Term, and Cash Offer

Category	Current	Option 1	Option 2	Option 3
Payments	$2,002	$1,629	$1,695	$1,812
Debt/loan amount	$186,116	$241,259	$227,342	$208,011
Term	27 Years	25 Years	20 Years	15 Years
Payment reduction	N/A	$373	$307	$190
Term reduction	N/A	2 Years	7 Years	12 Years
Cash	N/A	$55,134	$41,226	$21,895

In every option both the payment and term declined, in some cases significantly, while the cash went up. Choosing the right payment can make a huge difference in the benefits to the loan! By altering the payments, we can modify our benefits between payment reduction, term reduction, and cash. There are an infinite number of other scenarios that these principles can apply to, but ultimately, the perfect combination will depend on your situation and desires.

Payment Deferral (Short-term Payment Savings)

There is one additional, and substantial, payment benefit that can only be achieved through a mortgage refinance. It is called the payment deferral benefit. It is the savings you create by delaying, or *deferring*, your payments on debt that you are consolidating for the thirty-day period right after the loan closes. How does it work?

Let's look at our ongoing example one more time. The Hunters had $186,116 in total debt and were paying a combined monthly payment of $2,002. They paid off all of the debt through their mortgage refinance with a 6.5 percent rate.

The new mortgage loan was finalized and disbursed on June 25. The lender sent all the checks to the creditors and all the debts were paid off by July 1. The new payment for the loan is not due for thirty days, or August 1. The payments that would have been due on the debts, had they not refinanced and paid them off, would have been due periodically throughout July, but are now paid off. In essence, the borrower makes no payments to anyone for the entire month of July. Due to the fact that their previous payments totaled $2,002, that creates an additional $2,002 in savings!

There is one caveat to the deferral being true savings—you must reduce the term on the refinance from the existing mortgage term. If you extend it, you are not removing the payments, just extending them. You will save the payments in the short term, but you will give them back in the long term. By reducing the term, you are saving at both ends and the deferral savings is a true savings you do not give back later!

One final note: The more debt you consolidate and pay off, the more money you save in the deferral. In addition, if you are past due on any payments, by including them in the refinance, you not only save the amount of the monthly payments, but the amount of all past due payments. Remember, you would have had to pay them out of pocket at some point.

Can Anyone Get These Kinds of Benefits?

Every situation is different. Generally, there are three primary requirements to create the opportunity for these kinds of options and benefits. (There are a host of other qualifications needed to obtain approval for a loan; we will cover

qualifications in greater detail in chapter 10.) Those three requirements are:

1. You must have available equity to borrow against.
2. You must have a debt-to-payment relationship (DPR)
   that indicates you are paying too much on your debt.
3. You must have the income to afford the loan.

The bottom line is the more debt and equity you have, the
more payment-reduction, cash-availability, tax-savings, and
term-reduction opportunities you will likely have. If you do
not have equity, personal debt, or the income to afford the debt,
your options will be limited or may be none.

What If I Have No Debt?

If you have no debt other than your current mortgage loan,
a mortgage refinance that shortens your term or increases your
cash will always increase your payments, unless you reduce
your interest rate. With a rate reduction, you may be able to
create payment reduction, cash-out, and/or term reduction
benefits even without having and including personal debt.

Here is an example from the Hunters' previous scenarios
using the remaining mortgage balance only and leaving the
consumer debt out of the equation. (The customer's mortgage
balance was $144,126 at an interest rate of 6.0 percent with
twenty-seven years remaining on an original thirty-year loan;
we have rounded the loan amount to $146,000 to include nor-
mal fees.):

Category	Current	Option 1	Option 2	Option 3
Payments	$899	$784	$853	$899
Debt/loan amount	$144,126	$146,000	$146,000	$153,783
Term	27 Years	30 Years	25 Years	25 Years
Payment reduction	N/A	$115	$46	$0
Term reduction	N/A	+ 3 Years	2 Years	2 Years
Cash	N/A	$0	$0	$7,783

In this scenario all three options are at the lower interest rate of 5.0 percent. Why? Because in a rate and term refinance, with no additional cash-out or debt consolidation, the only way to improve your situation is by reducing your rate. Now, you may be thinking that if rate is not the primary consideration, why would someone need to lower their rate to create the benefits? Remember, rate matters when two loans are identical. Therefore, if you are refinancing your existing loan without adding cash or any other debt payments into the equation, you are comparing two like loans and need to reduce the rate to create benefits. And if you are adding cash or reducing term, there is simply no way to reduce your payments without reducing your rate because there are no additional personal debt payments to leverage.

However, you will note two important things. First, we did not need to reduce the interest rate by the full 2 percent rule we covered earlier in order for the refinance to make sense. Second, the traditional thirty-year term refinance that creates the greatest payment reduction, which is the most common one chosen, is actually the option that saves the least.

With as little as a 1 percent reduction in the rate, and even after the costs for the loan of $1,874, a rate and term refinance makes sense, but *only* if you choose options 2 or 3 (a reduction of two years or a reduction of two years with a cash out of about $8,000). Why? First, although option 1 saves you the most monthly, it extends your term and wipes out the savings in the long term. Second, even if you only consider the short-term savings and plan to move in a couple of years, it takes 16.3 months of savings just to pay back the fees and costs to break even (based on the estimated fees of $1,874 used). Finally, because the interest rate reduced, the interest deductions diminished, increasing your taxes in most cases. (I will cover this more in chapter 7.)

Option 2, although not the best option, reduces both the payments and term immediately. The benefits are not overwhelming, but are present. Option 3, which is the best option, matches your payment but reduces your term by two years and gives you $7,783 in cash. Even after the fees, that is a net cash value of $5,909 for the same monthly payment at a reduced term!

Again, every situation is different. The ultimate answer will lie in your situation and simply looking at your options from a different perspective than the age-old thirty-year rate and term refinance. Any option is generally better than that!

An important note about your payment amount: Although maximizing your monthly payment potentially optimizes the other benefits, we *never* want to choose a payment we cannot afford! This can lead to long-term cash flow problems that could result in delinquency and even foreclosure in extreme cases. (We'll discuss this in detail in chapter 10.)

Making the Right Payment in a Purchase Transaction

Now let's look at the importance of payment when purchasing a home. Because the payment directly correlates to the amount of home you will be able to buy, it is imperative that you choose the right payment to create the right benefits. Choosing the right payment is not only critical in determining the benefits gained through the home purchase, but also the ability to repay the mortgage on a timely basis. Before choosing a payment, we need to consider all of the benefits or detriments, and we must completely understand our cash flow. We do this by developing a budget so we get a payment that optimizes our benefits while not creating a burden to our cash flow.

Payment Is Usually a Dangerous Proposition in Home Buying!

Earlier I said that we usually choose the worst possible payment during purchase and refinance transactions. Let's look closer at why this is true in a purchase transaction by looking at the traditional scenario of a home purchase.

First, we determine the home price we want to start at. (Unfortunately it is rarely the price we end at!) Once determined, we start the process of looking at homes in that price range. Notoriously, we end up in the higher end of the range because the homes are much nicer and have more of the things we "need." Before long, we are looking at more and more expensive homes until we find one we emotionally fall in love with. Now that we have found the "home of our dreams," we start the process of seeing if we can qualify for financing.

Because of the aggressive nature of many of the lending programs out there, we end up getting approved for a larger loan than is prudent for our circumstances. In addition, we sometimes have to come up with more money down than we had originally planned. So we cash in savings and investments to scrape up the funds to qualify for the larger loan. The loan and home are both more than we originally had planned for, but all of the rationalization begins and we convince ourselves we can afford it. After all, it *is* our dream house, and the lender would not have approved the loan if we could not handle it!

Brian Tracy, author of several great books, including *The Psychology of Selling*, has a great saying that applies here: "People seldom buy logically; instead they buy emotionally and then defend it with logic!" How true and how dangerous! We end up getting a loan at the longest possible term, sometimes with rates that adjust to get the lowest possible payment, and have to get a program with a high debt-to-income ratio (as high as 50 percent or more) to qualify. Then, to add insult to injury, we put the greatest amount of money down we can, often draining any savings, investments, and emergency funds we had. All of this in an effort to have that dream home.

The result: We have a payment we can barely afford—for the longest possible term—with a potential of it going up, and no room for error. By doing this, not only do we potentially extend our debt past our planned retirement date, but we see no principal reduction to our mortgage for many years to come. As a result, we create no short-term equity in our home, unless the property value increases, and, worst of all, have no cash in reserves should we get in trouble. We got a great home . . . but have never been in worse financial shape!

Reverse Your Thinking Today!

Never approach a home from the standpoint of the value first and then work backward to the payment. Instead, first establish how much money is available to comfortably put down without depleting cash reserves and creating financial risk. Next, establish the *maximum affordable payment*, or MAP, for your short-term cash flow based on your budget. Last, establish the *maximum term* to achieve long-term debt freedom and retirement goals. Based on these three criteria, you can work forward into a home value that is truly affordable without compromising your overall financial picture. Let's look at these three steps in detail.

Determine the Right Down Payment

It is imperative that we decide on our down payment amount *before* determining the value of the home we are going to buy. In doing so, we can make an unbiased decision based on what funds we actually have that are reasonably available without the pressure of trying to meet a lender or lifestyle parameter. The key is not putting yourself at financial risk.

◇◇◇

We never want to be without cash reserves to draw on for emergency purposes or dip into retirement or college funds to use as a down payment on a home.

◇◇◇

If you deplete cash reserves, a change in the market that reduces the value of your home could literally wipe out your financial stability. In addition, the penalties for doing so could cost thousands. Use funds for down payments that are from sources such as bonuses, gifts, or savings and investments that were earmarked for use in purchasing a home. Once you have purchased your first home, the best down payment plan is rolling the appreciation you gain from the sale of your home, if any, into the next home. By continuing to do this every time you sell and purchase, you may be able to build a substantial down payment out of your equity. This will allow you to make down payments without affecting your investments or using money out of pocket. Finally, never be pressured into increasing the amount to "buy something better."

Always hold back a cash reserve for emergencies. I would recommend at least six months (preferably one year) of mortgage payments as a minimum starting point, if possible. This is a goal and may not seem feasible, but it is important that we create some type of emergency fund before venturing into a mortgage transaction.

Determine the Maximum Affordable Payment (MAP)

When navigating, we need a map. A map helps guide us to our ultimate destination without getting lost or in trouble. In navigating a home purchase, we want to determine our maximum affordable payment. This MAP helps us get to our ultimate destination, free and clear homeownership, without running into trouble. In the mortgage world, trouble is spelled f-o-r-e-c-l-o-s-u-r-e. This is something we want to stay far away from—your MAP is your rudder for staying out of dangerous waters!

Be careful! There are mortgage loan programs out there that allow upwards of 50 percent debt-to-income (DTI) ratios to qualify. This is far too aggressive for most people. A good conservative rule of thumb is to never have a mortgage payment (including any escrows for property taxes, homeowners insurance, or mortgage insurance) that exceeds 30 percent of your gross income (referred to as the "front-end DTI"), and a total DTI including *all* recurring debt payments of more than 35 percent (referred to as the "back-end DTI"). A front-end DTI of 25 percent and a back-end DTI of 30 percent is even more advisable. Here's a typical example:

$7,500 Monthly Gross Income x 30% DTI =
$2,250 Maximum Affordable Payment (MAP)

The key is getting a MAP we can *comfortably afford.* I would caution you to heed the 30 percent rule. It's best to be conservative in determining your MAP. We should never buy more house or take on more payment than is needed or affordable; the result can be devastating. However, we want to maximize our payment so that we can get the most cash at the shortest term possible to improve both the investment and the long-term cost. Considering our short-term cash flow is critical in this process, as it dictates the affordable payment and the long-term impact it is going to have!

DID YOU KNOW?

Determining our MAP requires that we include the costs for property taxes, homeowners insurance, and any other required insurance including private mortgage insurance. I recommend an escrow account as part of your monthly mortgage payment. An escrow is simply a reserve for these costs that the lender manages and includes in your monthly mortgage payment. Escrow these costs in the payment and calculate your maximum affordable payment (MAP) accordingly.

Using Your MAP to Determine Your Maximum Purchase Price

Now that you have established your MAP, it is time to determine your *Maximum Purchase Price*. The first step in this process is to calculate a maximum mortgage amount to determine the amount of accessible cash, based on our MAP and the maximum term you have chosen. This will ultimately affect the amount of home you can purchase. Let's look at an example. We are going to use the $2,250 MAP that was calculated earlier. By calculating the MAP at the going interest rate of 7.0 percent for different terms, we see a range of different loan (cash) amounts. (The following chart is a non-escrow sample. If you are including an escrow, you must make allowances for that in your MAP.)

Category	Option 1	Option 2	Option 3	Option 4
Maximum affordable payment (MAP)	$2,250	$2,250	$2,250	$2,250
Interest rate	7.0%	7.0%	7.0%	7.0%
Term	30 Years	25 Years	20 Years	15 Years
Loan amount (cash)	$338,192	$318,345	$290,210	$250,325

Although we can certainly get the most cash in option 1, we have to stretch all the way to a thirty-year term to get it. Depending on age, retirement plans, and long-term debt freedom goals, this is most likely not the best scenario. Always choose the *maximum term* that provides the lowest payment *without* exceeding your long-term retirement or debt-free plans (I'll cover this in greater detail in Chapter 7). Choosing a more moderate loan amount that leads to a less expensive home, but a mortgage with a shorter term, may fit our long-term objectives better, particularly if we can invest in improvements to the home that, over time, make it our dream home. Now we have created the best of all worlds: an affordable payment with a moderate term that meets our debt-free objectives and a place that we love.

Once we determine the maximum loan amount, the next step is to add the down payment to establish the maximum purchase price. As an example, if we had $30,000 cash that we had accumulated to put down on the purchase of our home, and we were settled with the payment and term in option 3 (approximately $290,000), we would have a maximum purchase price of $320,210:

Maximum Affordable Payment (MAP)	Interest Rate/ Term	Maximum Mortgage Amount	Down Payment	Maximum Purchase Price
$2,250	7.0%/ 20 years	$290,210	$30,000	$320,210

Of course, we would have to make sure that we deducted any loan costs out of this amount, and adjust for any escrows or tax and insurance costs, as discussed earlier. We would also have to be sure that our down payment amount meets the lender requirements for the maximum mortgage amount. Our lender can tell us what those requirements are. If not, we would want to adjust the maximum purchase price down to compensate.

Remember, this is the maximum loan amount based on your payment and term requirements and your maximum purchase price. It can always be less, but never more! Whatever the final purchase price becomes, the key is to *never exceed the*

*maximum down payment, maximum term, or MAP in your
ultimate purchase.*

Payment Is Clearly a Critical Consideration!

The payment amount in a mortgage transaction is a major
consideration that can provide substantial benefits if chosen
properly. We need to be careful to make our payment choices
based on how that payment will affect each of the other benefits and both our short- and long-term financial and life goals.
In doing so, we will optimize our payment benefit and start to
build a loan with true value!

NOTES

1. Do not confuse debt-to-payment relationship (DPR) with debt-to-
   income ratio (DTI). Remember, DPR is the relationship between your
   debt and payments, while DTI is the relationship between your *debt
   and income*. DPR tells you whether you are paying too much for your
   debt, while DTI tells you whether you can afford your debt. DPR tells you
   what you can *save* from a refinance, while DTI tells you whether you can
   qualify for a refinance.
2. The actual term reduction, and savings, is most likely even greater
   than the chart shows. The credit card debts were asterisked because
   the terms used were *estimates*, not actual. Credit card debt, also known
   as *revolving debt*, does not have a fixed term or payback. To create a
   payback comparison, we had to convert the debt from revolving to installment by taking the current balances, at the current interest rates,
   based on the current payments and calculating the remaining term.

   To accomplish this, we had to make three assumptions: (1) The balances will never increase (no future advances); (2) the payments will
   never change; and (3) the rate will never change. We can be certain that
   the terms and payback will be more than the assumptions we used unless

the borrower never used these credit cards again, and paid the same exact payment amount every month until the balances were paid off, and the lender never changed the rate or terms of the credit card. The likelihood of these three conditions is virtually nonexistent.

FINDING HIDDEN CASH IN YOUR
Home

B y now you probably realize there is a lot more to mortgages than just purchasing a home or refinancing at a lower rate. A mortgage, when used properly, can be much more than that. It can be the greatest investment you ever make, as it can also help you quickly achieve key savings goals, including retirement, emergency savings, or college funds for your children. Converting our home's equity into cash can, in certain cases, help us to achieve both our short- and long-term financial goals. *However, if done wrong, using your equity to access cash can also be the worst choice we can make and have devastating effects. The key is achieving equity protection and term reduction,* which ultimately accelerates debt elimination. In this chapter I will address both the pros and cons of this in detail. It is imperative that you consider your personal situation and the current market conditions before ever considering borrowing from your equity, and not do so unless it clearly improves your overall financial well-being. The cash value (equity) of your home can be accessed through a mortgage refinance or home purchase by choosing the right loan-to-value amount of a mortgage during a home purchase.

"Money for Nothing"

Think about the scenarios we used in chapter 5 when we looked at the impact of payment to both cash and term. In the example, the borrowers were originally paying $2,002 monthly for their $186,116 debt with twenty-seven years remaining on their mortgage term. Without changing their payments one cent, by simply converting their total debt into one fixed-rate, fixed-term mortgage loan, they freed up $110,385 in additional cash while still cutting their current mortgage term by two years. Kind of reminds you of that 1980s song "Money for Nothing," by Dire Straits, doesn't it? It's like getting money for nothing!

Our Equity May Be Our Greatest Resource for Cash

Believe it or not, our equity can actually be one of the greatest *investment vehicles* available for achieving our financial life goals. Because the equity in our home can represent the greatest asset we ever have for accessing cash, we want to consider utilizing it for cash purposes when looking at a mortgage loan. Borrowing against your equity to get cash can be very beneficial.

For example, the Pattersons have $75,000 in equity over and above the loan amount needed to pay off their mortgage and debts. At the same time, in looking at their current retirement savings, Jim Patterson realizes he has a severe shortage. He's forty-five and wants to retire at age sixty. He has been putting $7,500 per year into a 401(k) retirement plan for the past ten years. With an average return of 5.0 percent, he now has $99,051 in his retirement fund. That same investment carried out for the next fifteen years will yield $375,851 in cash value. However, based on a 3.1 percent inflation rate, the after inflation value is only $237,758.

Seems like a lot of money until Jim realizes that if he lives a decade past his retirement age of sixty—a likely scenario for most men—the money could quickly run out, particularly due to the rising cost of living. Therefore, Jim needs to increase his investments to get them to a sufficient level to comfortably support many more years of living. But he does not want to use up his equity, extend his term any longer, or increase his payments too much.

The Pattersons are looking to refinance their mortgage on a rate and term refinance. They borrowed $255,000 two years ago on a thirty-year term and have a current balance of $249,632 at a rate of 7.0 percent. Rates are now at 6.0 percent and their home is worth $406,000. At an 80 percent loan-to-value they have $325,000 in available equity—plenty to qualify for the loan. At a term of thirty years for a rate of 6.0 percent, their new mortgage payment will be $1,499, a savings of $198 a month.

In addition, Jim and his wife, Linda, have $25,000 in personal credit card debt they are paying $625 per month on (about 2.5 percent of the balances). Therefore, their total monthly payments including the personal debt payments, after refinancing, will be $2,124. Jim and Linda's plan is to stop using the credit cards and maintain the $625 payment every month on the personal debt until paid off, in hopes of getting debt free sooner.

Jim and Linda will end up with thirty years of mortgage payments and the personal debt payments until paid off. At an average interest rate of 13 percent for the credit cards, provided they followed their plan and never used them again (which is highly unlikely), their credit cards would be paid off in 4.4 years (53 months at $625 each month). Jim is convinced they have a sound plan for reducing their monthly mortgage payment and eliminating their debt. But there is a much better plan . . .

Instead of simply refinancing the mortgage to another thirty-year term and trying to manage the personal debt, by tapping into the full 80 percent equity available, the Pattersons could instead convert the remaining $75,000 in lendable equity into *cash*. This cash could pay off the personal debt and still leave $50,000 to invest. By doing so on a twenty-five-year term loan, they would decrease the term by five years *immediately*. And although their mortgage payment would increase by compressing payments into twenty-five years, their total payments *would decline*. Let's take a look at a comparison between the two loans:

Category	Current Situation	Rate and Term Refinance	Cash Out Refinance
Mortgage amount	$249,632	$250,000	$325,000
Mortgage payment	$1,697 @ 7.0%	$1,499 @ 6.0%	$2,094 @ 6.0%
Term	28 Years Remaining	30 Years	25 Years
Personal debt	$25,000	$25,000	$0
Personal debt payments	$625	$625	$0
Total payments*	$2,322	$2,124	$2,094
Payment difference	N/A	($198)	($228)
Term difference	N/A	+ 2 Years	(3 Years)
Cash	$0	$0	$50,000

*The personal debt payback portion was figured on a $625 payment for the $25,000 debt at an average rate of 13 percent.

By including the personal debt into the mortgage and leveraging the payments for that debt, Jim and Linda were able to lower their total payments by $228 up front ($30 more payment reduction than the combined rate and term refinance payment and existing personal debt payments) *and* reduce the existing mortgage loan term three years (five years less than with the rate and term refinance). More important, they were able to immediately access $50,000 additional cash for retirement! In case you are wondering whether the cash-out refinance makes sense in the long term from a total payback, the answer is yes.

What about an Adjustable Rate Mortgage?

You may have noticed that I am focusing primarily on fixed-rate, fixed-term mortgages. The reason is twofold. First, using fixed-rate, fixed-term examples when comparing creates less confusion. Second, I always prefer the stable nature of a fixed mortgage over an adjustable or interest-only mortgage.

Adjustable rate mortgages (ARM) and interest-only mortgages (I/O) were two of the major factors in the mortgage meltdown we have referred to many times, especially short-term initial adjustments (two- or three-year adjustments) and what is called an "Option ARM." The reason these were so devastating is that the short-term loans adjusted right in the midst of an aggressively increasing rate market and decreasing real estate market. As for the Option ARMs, they provided interest-only options that helped to qualify people for loans they could not afford and gave an option for interest only that eliminated debt reduction. These are both products that I would recommend you stay away from (or products like these that may come out in the future).

There is a benefit to and a place for an adjustable rate mortgage. The primary benefit to an ARM is a lower rate for the initial term in comparison to a fixed-rate loan. This certainly can make sense, but only under two conditions: (1) if you know that you will not get caught in a situation where the rate increases later and wipes out any savings you gained, or (2) the savings earned during the initial period is greater than the increased cost afterward.

For example, if you know you will move in three years, a five- or seven-year ARM can make sense. The key is getting out before the change takes away your savings. Therefore, make sure that you choose an ARM that adjusts *safely after* a date that you will be out of the home (sale or relocation). Never base the decision for an ARM on a plan to refinance at a later date, because circumstances could change—none of us knows what the future holds.

Finally, avoid interest-only loans, as it is just too easy to pay the interest-only option and lose any principal reduction. This will not help you to achieve debt elimination and freedom.

What about a Home Equity Loan or Line of Credit Instead?

Throughout this book we have focused primarily on first mortgage financing. Most of the benefits and principles we have mentioned apply to any kind of mortgage financing, including second mortgages—home equity loans or home equity lines of credit (HELOCs).

A second mortgage loan could certainly be another option for accessing the cash, but it is important you take the right kind of second mortgage loan and configure it in the right way.

We will look at the benefits and detriments of second mortgage loans in much greater detail in chapter 8.

Borrowing Against Your Equity—Helpful or Harmful?

You may be asking yourself several questions, including: *Is it really wise to borrow against my equity? Shouldn't I save my equity for an emergency? What about the increase in payments? What if I want to sell later; won't I be upside down in my equity?* These are all important and valid questions.

There are many who would, and do, advise you to *never* use your equity for borrowing cash. There is sound wisdom in their thinking when you consider the reasons why they are giving that advice. The reason is, very simply, to protect your equity.

There are many of you who, no matter what the benefits may be, are simply not comfortable borrowing against your equity and prefer to be debt free as soon as possible. I applaud you for that decision and congratulate you if you have saved money in a way that allows you to do that and achieve your financial goals! I will even address ways to pay down your mortgage and eliminate your debt faster through a *reverse investment philosophy* in chapter 7. I wholeheartedly agree with both of those objectives and will actually show you how to accomplish both when borrowing against your equity. What I want to teach you in this chapter is a revolutionary approach to achieving this.

As you have seen by now, getting out of debt is a core philosophy of this book. It is one of the best things you can do for yourself and your family—not just for the financial reasons, but also the personal reasons. Debt adds undue stress, pressure, and worries to life. It affects our attitude, our health, and our relationships. Being debt free is of vital importance—a goal all of us should make a top priority. Indeed, the book of Proverbs warns us about the burden of debt: "Just as the rich rule the poor, so the borrower is servant to the lender."[1]

Throughout this book, we have showed you multiple debt-elimination strategies. Although not borrowing is clearly the best strategy, for many that is simply not an option. Important and necessary financial needs may require access to cash we cannot get through any other way but our home's equity. In those cases, debt can be eliminated by maximizing payment and minimizing term, not by simply avoiding borrowing. There can be substantial financial benefits to using your equity . . . especially when you may be able to convert payments and debts into cash you don't have.

Our equity may be our greatest resource for cash. Using equity to access cash can be a great financial decision if done right. Therefore, it can be prudent to look at how we can access cash through our equity. The key is to borrow with a mind-set geared toward short-term repayment to eliminate the debt quickly.

Not using our equity to get additional cash simply because we don't want to might cause us to miss a great opportunity for financial independence. Why? Because equity is a *dormant* asset until you convert it into a *liquid* asset. There are only two ways to do that: Sell your home or pull out cash through a mortgage loan. Remember, equity, like everything else, can be here today and gone tomorrow.

Contrary to popular and traditional thinking, borrowing against your equity can be one of the best investment choices you can make if done properly.

◇◇◇

The key to borrowing against your home's equity is to use the cash so that it grows and pays for itself, offsets the costs, and still accelerates the payback on your mortgage to get you debt free sooner.

◇◇◇

Put simply, you must use the cash for the right purposes at the right term. This is what we call the *Equity Asset Return Now* principle—EARN!

Equity Asset Return Now—EARN!

When done properly, borrowing against your equity can yield cash for investments that will increase your wealth while paying for itself. And as you borrow, you can actually protect your equity and optimize the equity in your home in any market condition.

I realize that it could seem that by borrowing to access cash, we would increase our payments and reduce our equity, potentially putting us in a vulnerable situation. In addition, paying interest on money borrowed for investing would seem to cost more overall than we would gain. **If not done right, all of these things are true**. *But if done correctly*, you can acheive the following:

Equity: Your equity can be converted to a cash asset.

Asset: Your cash asset can be invested for growth.

Return: Your return on investment can outweigh the cost of borrowing.

Now: Your equity can be protected now.

That is the power of EARN!

Equity and Asset Protection

One of the main reasons for cashing in your equity is equity protection. The equity in your home is a major asset that needs protection. Let's learn from the real estate bust that started in 2006 and continues as of this writing. How many people thought the equity in their homes was "secure" only to lose tens or hundreds of thousands in that equity when the real estate values tanked? Because they did not capitalize on their equity, they missed the opportunity to get at the cash value. The only way to get that equity back is to wait for the home's value to return. The problem is that no one knows when, or if, that will happen and to what level. The unfortunate fact is that the equity was there but never cashed in because homeowners were not educated on the right way to use equity. I hope that will change through this book.

We cannot rely on equity to always build and home values to always climb. As the Bible warns, we are "not to trust in our money, which is so unreliable."[2]

Now you may be thinking, *Wasn't overly aggressive borrowing and tapping into equity for cash part of the problem?* Aggressive borrowing and tapping into equity for cash for *the wrong reasons* was the real problem.

This principle of cashing in equity as an asset is similar to cashing in stocks when they have greatly appreciated. Years ago a friend who owned technology stock options worth over one million dollars approached me in church on a Sunday morning. He told me how well the stocks had done and said his options were coming due. He asked my advice: "Should I convert them or let them continue to grow?"

Knowing that stocks had been increasing for a long period

of time and had a good chance of reversing, I told him, "Cash it in!" He continued to tell me about its worth if it continued at the pace it was going for the next six months.

Now, I would never tell anyone to leave church, but I told him that if he had to do that to cash it in, he should do it now! He didn't know whether the stock price was going up or down, and neither did I. What he did know was its value today. I also knew he earned about $85,000 per year, so his stocks represented more than fifteen years of income. "You probably won't make that much the rest of your career. Sell it now and never look back!"

He didn't leave church. He didn't sell his stock options. He didn't cash it in. By the time he sold the stock, the entire options were worth only $27,000.

◇◇◇

Equity, just like stock, is worth nothing until you cash it in.

◇◇◇

Equity works exactly the same way. It's a dormant asset. Your equity is worth nothing to you unless you use it. To convert it from a dormant asset to a liquid asset, you have to cash it in. This is a principle the majority of people miss. The key here is cashing it in for the *right purposes*, with the *right direction* and advice, in the *right kinds of conservative investments* that protect your equity while increasing the value of the asset.

What if you had to sell your home and, because you borrowed against the equity to get the cash, you are now "upside down" on the equity? Wouldn't you be in terrible shape and be blocked from selling? Actually, you could be in much better shape. How? By simply pulling the principal amount you borrowed back out of your investment and applying it to your mortgage balance. This would put you in the same equity position you would have been in while letting you retain any profit earned from the investment. Even as a last resort, if you end up paying taxes plus a 10 percent penalty for withdrawing the funds in certain situations, although not desirable, you still would be better off than losing 100 percent of your equity!

Return (Offsetting the Cash Cost)

Think about the example of the Pattersons. What happens if they take the $50,000 cash and invest it at a 5.0 percent rate of return? What would be the cost for borrowing the cash and then the return on the investment?

Category	Current Situation	Cash-Out Refinance
Mortgage amount	$249,632	$325,000
Mortgage payment	$1,697 @ 7.0%	$2,094 @ 6.0%
Cash	$0	$50,000
Term	28 Years Rem.	25 Years
Personal debt	$25,000	$0
Personal debt payments	$625	$0
Total payments	$2,322	$2,094
Payment difference	N/A	($228)
Cash portion of payment	N/A	$322
Annual cost for cash	N/A	$3,864
Life of loan cost for cash	N/A	$96,600

The new mortgage payment for the twenty-five-year term is $2,094. The portion of the Pattersons' monthly payment for the $50,000 cash included in the loan is $322, or $3,864 annually. Therefore, the total payment cost for the additional

$50,000, over the life of the loan, would be $96,600: $322 monthly payment portion x 300 payments = $96,600.

Now, let's look at what the return would be for the $50,000 investment. The chart "Returns for $50,000 Investment from a Mortgage" details the cost and return of the Pattersons' $50,000 investment at key points during the twenty-five years of the mortgage:

Returns for $50,000 Investment from a Mortgage

Year	Annual Payment Cost	Cumulative Payment Cost	Annual Investment Return	Cumulative Investment Return	Cumulative Investment Value	Cumulative Gain
0	0	0	0	0	$50,000	$50,000
1	$3,864	$3,864	$2,500	$2,500	$52,500	$48,636
2	$3,864	$7,728	$2,625	$5,125	$55,125	$47,397
3	$3,864	$11,592	$2,756	$7,881	$57,881	$46,289
4	$3,864	$15,456	$2,894	$10,775	$60,775	$45,319
5	$3,864	$19,320	$3,039	$13,814	$63,814	$44,494
10	$3,864	$38,640	$3,879	$31,445	$81,445	$42,805
15	$3,864	$57,960	$4,949	$53,946	$103,946	$45,986
18	$3,864	$69,522	$5,730	$70,331	$120,331	$50,809
19	$3,864	$73,416	$6,017	$76,348	$126,348	$52,932
20	$3,864	$77,280	$6,317	$82,665	$132,665	$55,385
25	$3,864	$96,600	$8,063	$119,318	$169,318	$72,718

Notice that the total interest accumulated for the twenty-five-year investment was $119,318—over double the amount invested! This increases the total value of the $50,000 investment to $169,318—over triple. When you subtract the $96,600 total cost of the payments for the twenty-five years from the total investment value of $169,918, you net a $72,718 return on investment before taxes!

As you can see, the annual interest earned is higher than the annual payments in year 10 and the cumulative interest earned is greater than the cumulative annual payments in year 18. You may be thinking that means it takes eighteen years to break even. Actually, it does not—you are gaining from the very start. Why?

Remember, the Pattersons were already paying $2,322 in total payments for at least the next 4.4 years. (That is when we estimated the personal debt would be fully paid.) The $50,000 cash was included in their new payment of $2,094, which was $228 less than their current payments. Therefore, there really was no initial cost for the $50,000, because it was included in the lower payment at the lesser term of twenty-five years.

The $3,864 we show in the previous chart represents the portion of the Pattersons' new payment from the cash, but they were already paying more than that anyway. They did not borrow an additional $50,000 over their payments, but converted their current payments to *include* the cash. Remember, their net payments went down and their term got shorter; therefore, the cash that was included cost virtually nothing, initially.

Unlocking Tax Benefits in Your Home

In addition, by borrowing the additional funds and increasing their loan size, the Pattersons may have gained a tax deduction benefit from the additional mortgage interest created by the larger loan. Although we discussed taxes in detail in chapter 3, let's take a closer look at how tax benefits affected the Pattersons' loan. Recall from the chart "Returns for $50,000 Investment from a Mortgage" that the Pattersons had a cumulative gain, or investment return, over the twenty-five years of

$72,718 before taxes.

By borrowing the additional $50,000, the Pattersons' annual payment cost for that portion of the loan was $3,864, or $96,600 for the twenty-five years. Look at the additional interest and tax savings created by borrowing that extra $50,000:

Cumulative Payment Cost	Cumulative Mortgage Interest	Tax Bracket	Life of Loan Tax Benefit	Cumulative Gain	Adjusted Gain
$96,600	$46,645	x 28%	$13,061	$72,718	$85,779

Of the $96,600 in total payments over the life of the loan, $46,645 was interest. Assuming the Pattersons kept the loan and the investment for the full twenty-five years and that 100 percent of the cash borrowed was tax deductible, by multiplying the interest by their tax bracket (as discussed in chapter 3) we find that the net tax savings for the twenty-five years is $13,061. That increases the return to $85,779 (adjusted gain).

Tax Benefits to Paying Off the Personal Debt

In addition to this tax benefit, the Pattersons also gained a potential tax benefit for the $25,000 they borrowed to consolidate the personal debt. Remember, interest paid on personal debt is not tax deductible, only mortgage interest is. Therefore, depending on the debts paid off and the tax laws in place at the time, they may be able to convert all of the personal debt into tax-deductible mortgage debt. The portion of the $2,094 payment used for debt consolidation was $161.08. Assuming again that 100 percent of the interest was deductible through their new mortgage loan, here is what the additional tax benefits for that portion would be (next page):

Tax Benefits from $25,000 for Debt Consolidation

Cumulative Payment Cost ($25,000)	Cumulative Mortgage Interest Paid	Tax Bracket	Life of Loan Tax Benefit ($25,000 Portion)	Life of Loan Tax Benefit ($50,000 Portion)	Total Life of Loan Tax Benefit
$48,323	$23,323	x 28%	$6,530	$13,061	$19,591

The tax savings the Pattersons gained over the life of the loan for the debt they consolidated, assuming a twenty-five-year term with no change in tax laws, is an additional $6,530. When adding that to the tax savings for investment, the total tax bene-fit, or savings, becomes $19,591 for the life of the loan. Clearly tax considerations are a major factor in the overall bene-fit and value of a mortgage loan.

Now let's look at a comparison between the total mortgage interest paid and tax benefits of the Pattersons' current loan and larger cash-out refinance loan.

Category	Amount	1st Year Interest Total	Tax Savings @ 28%
Current mortgage amount (7.0%)	$249,632	$17,768	$4,975
Current personal debt	$25,000	N/A	0
New mortgage amount (6.0%)	$325,000	$19,343	$5,416

In the first year of the Pattersons' new mortgage, although they are reducing their interest rate by 1.0 percent, by pay-ing off the personal debt that provides no interest deductions and adding the cash for investment, the tax benefits actually increase by $441 (assuming full tax deductibility on the new mortgage). If you compare the interest accumulations over the life of each loan, you will find that the interest deductions are greater for the cash-out refinance than the current situation in the first twenty-one years of the twenty-five-year term. The Pattersons begin to lose tax benefits only in the twenty-second year—when they are nearly out of debt!

Tax Offsets from Investments

In addition to considering the tax benefits, we must also consider the tax costs (when applicable) in determining the total value of the loan. Depending on the form of investment, use of any capital gains, etc., you may have to pay taxes on the investment. Using our example one more time, if the $50,000 was invested in a typical savings or money-market account or any non-retirement or non-education plan, there will be a capital gains tax or ordinary income taxes for the increased value of the investment.

However, by investing the proceeds from your loan (cash-out) into a *tax-deferred* 401(k) retirement fund or certain college funding plans (like a 529 plan), you can minimize these tax ramifications. (A tax-deferred investment is one where there is no tax that has to be paid on the earnings accumulated for the investment until the cash is withdrawn. At the point the earnings are used, they are taxed at the current income bracket of the owner.) Most college funding plans provide tax-free growth when the funds are used for education purposes.

To determine the net value of the tax savings, we would simply subtract the tax costs from the tax savings. I highly recommend you seek a qualified financial advisor for any mortgage transaction to help you clearly understand the tax impact, both the benefits and costs, of any mortgage or investment transactions you make.

Bottom line, by paying off non–tax deductible debt and accessing cash, thereby increasing the loan amount, we potentially increase our tax benefits. Additionally, the interest rate on a mortgage loan is almost always less than that of unsecured debt. When we build a loan that can decrease our overall payments, increase our cash, and reduce our taxes all at the same time, as we did with the cash-out debt consolidation, we are truly building a loan of great value.

What if I Invested the Money on My Own?

Imagine this was your loan and, instead of borrowing the $50,000 to invest, you took the $322 you would have saved monthly and simply invested it on your own. What would be the result? Would it be better or worse? The answer depends on you and your level of discipline.

By investing $322 every month for twenty-five years in the same 5.0 percent investment, the total value of the investment would be $193,638, which is $24,320 more than the value of the $50,000 invested over the same twenty-five years. The reason is simply the nature of accumulated earnings. However, you would lose the tax benefits created by financing the investment into the loan and increasing your mortgage interest deductions. Those deductions would total $13,061 over the life of the loan. Therefore, the net difference is $11,259 in savings achieved by investing on your own. That's not a great amount when you consider this is a twenty-five-year investment—it's an average of only $450 additional earnings per year—but certainly worth noting.

The real question is not could you have gained more, but would you? In other words, are you disciplined enough to make a $322 payment to your investment account every month for the next three hundred months to achieve that kind of investment return? This requires making the payment every month regardless of future earnings and events. This also means making it every thirty days, on the same date, without skipping a single payment. How many times have we tried to discipline ourselves to consistent behaviors in the past, only to eventually stop? Does saving, dieting, or exercise sound familiar?

The fact is, to make that kind of commitment and stick with it for three hundred straight months is statistically unlikely, no matter how disciplined we may be. Life just throws too many things at us that can take us off our plan.

Even though there is ultimately greater upside in investing the savings on your own, it is only slightly more. The risk that it won't happen is substantially high. By borrowing the money, investing it today, and including it in a mortgage payment, we are in essence creating a "forced" savings account. We know the money is there and growing. The chance that we will actually see the return for the investment, as planned, is more likely than trying to do it on our own month by month.

Ultimately, either investment option is better than doing nothing. Whether you converted the current payments to consolidate your debts, lower your payments, shorten your term, and then invest the payment savings to build your financial strength, or convert the current payments into $50,000 cash to do the same, you still would be in much better shape than leaving your debt, payments, and equity in its current state—dormant!

Whether you access cash out of your equity or not, using

your mortgage to reduce payments, term, and taxes and defer payments still makes great sense. Borrowing the cash for investing just adds another element of assurance to your future financial picture. It's ultimately your choice. However, keep in mind this important guideline no matter how or why you borrow to convert equity into cash:

◇◇◇

When you convert equity into cash, always do so at the shortest possible term you can afford to rebuild the equity in your home and eliminate your debt as quickly as possible.

◇◇◇

Bottom Line—Only Invest in Sound Investments!

There are three major caveats to keep in mind when drawing on your home equity:

First, you must invest in "sound investments." In the case of the Pattersons, the 5 percent investment return did not fluctuate. That average return can happen with stable investments, such as money market funds, certificates of deposit (CDs), and some conservative mutual funds. That kind of return may be possible with stable, sound investments, depending on the type of investment you choose and the market conditions at the time. Traditionally, investments in things like money market funds, certificates of deposit (CDs), Treasury securities, and some conservative mutual funds have been examples of this. However, on occasion, finding a sound investment may be difficult or even impossible—as we have seen through 2008 into early 2009. But in a stable market, opportunities exist for safe, sound investments. The key here is to work with a qualified financial expert to determine the safest possible investment at the time you access the cash that will ensure a positive return at the greatest possible yield available. *In addition, you must make sure that the institution(s) you are investing in are financially sound themselves.* Therefore, be sure to do your homework on the company you are investing in!

Second, only borrow cash for "investment and return" purposes. Unless you are independently wealthy and have unlimited cash reserves, I would recommend only using cash from your equity for investment and return purposes—in other words, purposes that act as an investment that creates a return. Although not traditionally considered an investment, borrowing to consolidate debt, when done properly as we have outlined in this book—to reduce payments, improve tax benefits, create term reduction, and provide payment savings through a deferral—is a great example of an investment use that gains a return. The more traditional uses of cash for investment would be any use that increases wealth or improves your financial situation. These could include

- purchasing a home or investment property that has a likely chance of increasing in value;
- investing—in *sound* investments with probable returns;
- improving property—home improvements that increase value (not all home improvements increase value and ensure a return on investment and for those that do, returns can vary depending on the improvement)[3]; or
- charitable causes that create tax shelters and, more importantly, intrinsically change the lives of others.

Cash for major purchases (cars, boats, etc.), vacations, gambling, risky investments, and so on are very dangerous. **Never put your home or your family in jeopardy by using your equity for these kinds of purposes.**

Third, nothing is guaranteed. Understand that when you are dealing with investments, *nothing* is ultimately guaranteed. We want to invest as soundly and conservatively as possible to enhance our chances of return and create stability in the investment. However, it is important to understand that there is no true guarantee for the future.

Beyond these three caveats, let me add one more: *Money does not ensure happiness.* I know this is an age-old saying, yet it is a truth we must embrace to have a truly satisfying and joyous life. I'll talk about this in much greater detail in the final chapter of this book (chapter 11).

A Key Caution in Using Your Home Equity

Nothing I have written in this chapter should be interpreted or construed as a recommendation to immediately cash in your equity for purposes of obtaining cash. This is simply a valid strategy worth consideration. As I have stated throughout this chapter, doing so can have detrimental effects. However, in certain situations (which we have discussed), I believe circumstances can sometimes warrant valid consideration for cashing in a portion of your equity. And knowing that utilizing equity to access cash has become a common practice in mortgage financing, the fact is that millions of people will do so in the coming years regardless of whether this book had been published or not. Therefore, I want to give those individuals who make that choice proper guidance and direction in the right way to do so.

The examples in this chapter speak for themselves and give compelling reasons to only do so for safe, sound investments. However, these are predicated on the return from the investment outweighing the cost of borrowing the funds and/or the loss in equity experienced by not cashing in the equity. Always seek out qualified financial and tax advice before borrowing against your equity for the purposes of getting cash. Also, be sure you are investing in not just sound *investments*, but sound *institutions*. Understand that no investment or investment return is "guaranteed."

Finally, never spend money you have borrowed on frivolous or unnecessary things; only borrow against your equity if it *clearly* improves your overall financial situation and security! Ultimately, borrowing against your equity is a very critical and personal choice, one based on your own beliefs. Many people, regardless of their situation, may simply choose not to use their equity as a tool for leveraging cash and that is certainly understandable. This is a decision you do not want to make lightly, but an option that may make dollars and good sense.

Cash in a Purchase Transaction—Reverse Cash Access

Until now, we have been talking about how to access cash in a refinance. What about a purchase? The primary use of cash in a purchase transaction is for the purchase of the home. Our hope is that we are investing in a home that appreciates and creates a substantial return on investment over time. Depending on the real estate market at the time of purchase, this may or may not be the case.

Although you cannot borrow against your equity directly in a purchase transaction, as you do not yet own the home, there is a "reverse method" for getting cash in a purchase transaction. This happens by maximizing the loan-to-value in the purchase, thereby minimizing the down payment amount. Some lenders offer programs that can exceed the standard 20 percent down payment required to avoid mortgage insurance. These may be available through higher loan-to-value (LTV) first mortgage programs (85, 90, or 95 percent) or combination programs where you combine a conventional first mortgage at 80 percent LTV with a second mortgage (home equity loan) or home equity line of credit (anywhere from 5 percent to 20 percent LTV depending on the lender programs).

The primary intention of a combination loan is to avoid paying mortgage insurance. The downside is that, in many cases, the interest rate for the second mortgage may be higher than the rate for the first mortgage. Although these programs are much less common than they used to be, they may still be available (depending on the lender and the market at the time). However, in many cases you will still have to pay mortgage insurance. Because every lender is different, you will have to talk to your lender about their guidelines. The benefit of the *reverse*

DID YOU KNOW?

The Homeowner's Protection Act (HPA) of 1998 grants you the right to request private mortgage insurance cancellation when you reach 20 percent equity in your mortgage. What's more, lenders are required to automatically cancel PMI coverage when a 78 percent loan to value is reached (although liens on the property or not keeping up with payments could require further PMI coverage). Be sure to cancel when you reach the proper equity level.[4]

cash access is access to more of the cash you would have used to put down on the house for investment-type purposes or emergency cash reserves.

By decreasing the down payment, four things can immediately happen:

1. You have use of the funds that would have been applied to the down payment.
2. On the down side, by decreasing the down payment, you increase the loan size, which increases the payment. In addition, as mentioned earlier, because you have less than the standard 20 percent down for mortgage financing, you may have to pay mortgage insurance (depending on the lender and the program available).
3. However, by investing the funds in a sound investment, you can earn interest on the funds to offset all or a portion of the payment increase (depending on the type of investment). The amount you will offset will completely depend on the overall return on the investment (determined by a combination of the yield and earnings on the investment, the length of time invested, and the tax costs).
4. In addition, by increasing the payment and loan size, you also increase the amount of interest you pay each year, which potentially increases the mortgage interest you pay and could deduct in your taxes. This, too, may offset a portion of the payment increase.

Look at it this way: A down payment is an investment. The primary reason for considering the reverse-cash-access method is that, depending on market conditions, it may be safer to retain the cash you planned to use for your down payment and invest it in a sound investment you can be confident in than put it into a home where the value drops and eliminates the investment.

Consider again the depressed real estate market and the depreciated values in 2006–2009 through most of the United States. Let's say you put $40,000 down (20 percent) on a $200,000. If the home depreciates, you could lose the entire investment. If instead, you could put just $20,000 down (10 percent) and retain the other $20,000 to put into a safe investment that earns some growth and tax benefits, even after the increased payment, you could protect the majority of your cash and even make a return (depending on the investment). In addition, you still have access to the cash and any earnings for an emergency fund.

Although the cash access and investment options are not as great in a purchase as in a refinance, there are valid reasons to consider converting down payment, just like equity, into cash.

Whether this is beneficial to you depends on the amount of interest you end up paying on the mortgage and earning on the investment, the ultimate tax benefits and costs of doing so, and the situation and market conditions at the time. Be sure to consult with a financial expert before determining whether using some of your down payment as an investment benefits your particular financial situation. Still, this may be another option worth looking into to retain your cash and invest it for future growth.

NOTES

1. Proverb 22:7.

2. 1 Timothy 6:17.

3. To learn what home improvements give the best return, check with a professional. Another good resource is the *Remodeling* magazine annual survey of real estate professionals to find out how much various projects can return to a home's value. For average costs and value recovered, see summary reported in *Consumer Reports*, September 2008, p.19.

4. Adapted from *The Money Alert,* www.themoneyalert.com/mortgage insurance.

5. Federal legislation passed in 2008 has made private mortgage insurance tax deductible, much like mortgage interest and property taxes. There are some restrictions, such as the property must be your primary residence, your adjusted gross income must be $100,000 or less for full deduction (partial deductions up to $109,000), and the origination of your mortgage must have occurred on or after January 1, 2007. Lawmakers have extended this private mortgage insurance tax deduction through 2010. Please consult a tax advisor regarding your specific situation. (Information from *The Money Alert*, July 3, 2008, on the Internet at www. themoneyalert.com/mortgageinsurance.html

CHAPTER SEVEN

TERM AS KEY TO FINANCIAL
Freedom

T erm, or the length of the mortgage, is perhaps the most significant component to getting a great mortgage and achieving financial freedom. As we have discussed throughout this book, we want to be debt free as soon as possible. Therefore, considering our long-term debt-free goals is a critical component to the mortgage transaction.

We can see the impact of term by revisiting the Hunters' scenario (from chapter 5). Recall that they had twenty-seven years and a $186,116 balance remaining on their 6.5 percent mortgage when they decided to refinance and reduce their monthly payment. They had a mortgage loan payment of $899 and other debt payments totaling $1,103 for combined payments of $2,002. Had they chosen to pay that same total payment on their refinance, they would have reduced their term on all of their debt to ten years, ten months. That is what I call the "matched payment option"—combining all monthly debt payments and the mortgage amount into one refinanced loan.

By matching the payment, the result is a 10.8-year term (as we showed you in chapter 5). By converting their payments into a mortgage refinance, without changing the payments one penny, the Hunters reduced the mortgage by 16.2 years, or 60 percent, and paid off all of the debt in less than eleven years! By choosing the matched payment approach, they achieved not only a much shorter mortgage term, but a substantial savings in payback.

Category	Current	Same Payment Option
Total debts (Mortgage plus personal)	$186,116	$186,116
Payments	$2,002	$2,002
Term	27 Years	10.8 Years
Term difference	N/A	(16.2 Years)
Term payback	$339,283	$259,456
Payback difference	N/A	($79,827)

Clearly, term has a profound impact on payback, or the total cost of the loan over time. Again, if this were your situation, the $79,827 in payback savings would be *your* savings. This money could either be spent on mortgage interest or used for long-term financial gain—it's your choice.

Term Option Availability

Although most lenders will not specifically offer a 10.8-year term, many offer loan terms in increments of five years, starting as low as ten, all the way up to thirty (some even have forty- and fifty-year terms—terms you should *never* consider). Choosing the right term is not only critical to payback savings, but also to retirement and debt-free planning. We will look deeper at this concept shortly when we explore the future retirement expense eliminator, or FREE.

One major rule for mortgage financing that I have discussed throughout this book is to *never extend the term you currently have on your existing mortgage if you can afford a shorter term loan.* Extending the term almost never makes sense, as it typically wipes out any savings you have created through payment reduction; you usually lose money in the long term! In the chart "Thirty-Year Rate and Term Refinance versus Twenty-Five-Year Debt Consolidation," you will find several scenarios of mortgage loans where the borrower refinanced to a thirty-year mortgage and maintained the personal debt. The final two columns of the chart show how a refinance to a twenty-five-year term including the debt balances affects the payments. In all cases, a twenty-five-year full debt consolidation refinance makes much better sense, usually saving hundreds of dollars in monthly payments compared with the thirty-year term refinance.

Thirty-Year Rate and Term Refinance versus Twenty-Five-Year Debt Consolidation

30-year Mortg. Balance	Rate	Mortg. Paymt.	Personal Debt Remaining	Personal Debt Paymt.[1]	Total Combined Paymt.	Consol. Debt Refi. (25 Yrs)	Paymt. Savings
			$10,000	$250	$787	$643	$144
$100,000	5%	$537	$25,000	$625	$1,162	$730	$432
			$50,000	$1,250	$1,787	$877	$910
			$10,000	$200	$1,780	$1,755	$25
$250,000	6.5%	$1,580	$25,000	$500	$2,080	$1,857	$223
			$50,000	$1,000	$2,580	$2,025	$555

Payment reductions occurred in every situation, even with as little as $10,000 in consumer debt. I even adjusted the personal debt payment calculation percentages to allow for lower or higher percentages. More importantly, the rate either increased or stayed the same in every case—once again proving that rate is not the most important consideration.

Term in a Purchase Transaction

The duration of the mortgage is just as important in a purchase as a refinance. *Term is the primary driver of the overall long-term costs of a mortgage.* The shorter the term, the less the interest costs over the life of the loan.

Which Would You Rather Pay?

A $250,000 home, if financed at a 6 percent interest rate, can cost you from as much as $539,595 to as little as $379,736, depending on the term you choose (see below).

Term	30 Years	25 Years	20 Years	15 Years
Loan amount	$250,000	$250,000	$250,000	$250,000
Payment	$1,499	$1,610	$1,791	$2,109
Interest payback	$539,595	$483,226	$429,859	$379,736
Difference	N/A	($56,369)	($109,736)	($159,859)

If you can afford the larger payments, why not commit to them? Remember, it's your money. The difference between the twenty- and thirty-year payments, for example, is only $292, but the difference in the interest payback is $109,736. This is money that could be applied to your future!

Time Is Harder to Get Back than Money

"Time is more valuable than money," the old saying goes. It's true—you can always get more money, but you can never get more time! For that reason, term consideration is not only important from the standpoint of the monetary savings, but also the age difference at payoff. The earlier you pay off your home and become mortgage free, the more you free up opportunities for living a long and fruitful retirement.

Let's look at some great tactics for reducing your term and becoming mortgage free sooner, whether you are purchasing a home or refinancing your mortgage.

Future Retirement Expense Eliminator (FREE)

How would you like to be FREE of all debt at retirement? How would you like to own your home free and clear and have no mortgage payment? How would you like to create a debt-free asset worth hundreds of thousands of dollars that could be used for helping fund your retirement? This is exactly what FREE—Future Retirement Expense Eliminator—is all about!

Before even considering a mortgage loan, the first thing we want to establish is our Debt Elimination Date, or DED (and we want it to be before we are dead!). This date may correlate directly to your retirement, or a date that is pre-retirement so you can use the money you would have been paying on your debt to help you build your wealth in the years leading up to retirement. In either case, your mortgage term should *never* exceed your debt elimination or planned retirement date. This is *always* the driving force behind the term you choose. Later in this chapter I will address what you should do if you are already at or near retirement, or cannot afford a shorter term later in this chapter.

Staying on Track for Your Debt Elimination Date (DED)

Whether you are refinancing or purchasing a home, the DED becomes an immovable target that you always focus on. Each time you refinance or purchase a new home, you use that date as your driver for the new term so that you always stay on track for being debt free. The beauty is, by establishing this date from the start, it forces you to choose short-term financing, which in turn creates faster principal reduction so you keep gaining on the term without having too dramatic of an impact on the payments. This is a foundational approach to financial freedom at or before retirement. Let me give you an example. Jeff is a thirty-five-year-old borrower buying his first home. Let's track a twenty-five-year plan for debt freedom:

A Debt-Free Home in Twenty-Five Years

Age	Type	Purch. Amt.	Loan Amt.	Term (Rem. Yrs.)	Pmt. (P&I)	Balance	Value Increase (3% per yr)	Value
35	Buy	$187K	$150K	25	$1,012	$142,000	$17,340	$204K
38	Refi	N/A	$170K	22	$1,212	$162,000	$12,444	$217K
43	Buy	$250K	$195K	20	$1,454	$180,000	$39,819	$290K
48	Refi	N/A	$220K	15	$1,916	$167,000	$46,161	$336K
53	Buy	$350K	$181K	10	$2,055	$105,000	$55,746	$406K
58	Refi	N/A	$125K	5	$2,445	Paid	$64,665	$471K

In this scenario we assumed a conservative annual appreciation of 3 percent and an interest rate of 6.5 percent. Jeff applied 100 percent of the appreciation gain from his home as a down payment on the next home (as we covered in chapter 6). In following this simple plan, Jeff and his family became mortgage free at their targeted DED and had a $471,000 free-and-clear asset. In addition, they accessed $88,000 cash in their three refinances.

Although this is a perfect-case scenario and there would

possibly be loan transaction and home sales costs to deduct, you can still get a picture of how powerful having, and sticking to, your DED becomes! Although the borrower's payments more than doubled, based on a 3 percent annual pay increase, his income would have nearly doubled and he would have realized thousands in tax savings also, offsetting the increase in payments.

If You're Already Retired or Cannot Afford a Shorter Term

What if you are already retired or very close to your desired retirement age? Do you still want to establish a DED? It's possible, and it depends on three important factors: your debt, your income, and your remaining financial goals.

Sam Ralla is fifty-seven and wants to retire at sixty-seven when he gets 100 percent of his pension. However, he cannot afford a ten-year refinance of his mortgage balance based on his current income. The payment would simply be too high and his income will drop at retirement. He wants to get out of debt as soon as possible to reduce his monthly outgo at retirement (when his income decreases) and pay off the mortgage so he can leave the home to his children debt free. He also would like to give $10,000 to his only grandchild, $10,000 to his church, and another $10,000 to his favorite charity.

Sam currently has seventeen years left on his thirty-year mortgage, which he took out for $130,000 at 6.5 percent. His current balance is $101,302, and his credit card balances total $12,100. He is paying $821 on his mortgage and $363 on his credit cards for a total of $1,184. If Sam refinanced his mortgage and credit cards at the same rate he has today on a fifteen-year term, he would actually reduce his term two years instantly and his total payments to $966—a $218 savings (this assumes $1,500 in fees and closing costs). If he then applied the $218 savings directly to his mortgage payment each month, he would be on track to pay off his mortgage balance in 11.8 years. As a result, his mortgage balance in ten years would be about $25,000 instead of $55,000. At this point he could sell the house, retain the $30,000 difference in added cash for the gifts he desired, and pay cash for a smaller home, making his free and clear.

Felix is seventy. He has ten years remaining on his mortgage of $85,950. He took it out twenty years ago for $150,000 at 7 percent. His current mortgage payments are $997. He also is paying $182 each month toward the $7,300 balance on his credit cards. He *has* retired, just recently, and things are very tight on his fixed income. Felix can afford his payment, and his income is stable, but he has little additional cash and little money put away in savings. Felix has lots of equity in his home but does not want to sell it even though he has been told he should to get the cash out of it. Felix has no heirs, so paying off his home is really not a concern to him. How can he stay in his home and still get additional cash?

This is the only scenario where increasing the term of the loan could make sense. Felix could refinance his mortgage and credit cards into a matched payment; with a new thirty-year loan, he can afford to live comfortably. What would happen? At 6.5 percent, he would get a loan of $186,530. That means he would pay off his debt, keep his payments the same, and access about $90,000 in cash after fees. This money could be put into a sound investment as a cash reserve that also earns interest, improving both his cash situation and annual earnings (assuming he takes the capital gains as earnings).

The key here is to retain plenty of equity in the property to be in a position to sell, if needed. A good rule of thumb in this situation is to not borrow more than 60 percent of the home's value to maintain a good cushion.

Other Term Reduction Strategies

In addition to the term reduction strategies we have already discussed—short-term focus, never extending your term, and establishing a DED—there are other ways to make an impact on your mortgage balance and term to accelerate the payoff, reducing interest payback on your mortgage loan.

Strategy #1: Biweekly Mortgage Payment Plans

Biweekly payment plans have become a popular tool over the past several years. Many mortgage loan officers use this as a tool to differentiate themselves and to show a reduced effective interest rate when trying to sell their customers a loan. Many companies have developed biweekly payment plans that customers can sign up for to handle the payments. The fact of the matter is that biweekly payments are available to any borrower; they are not something that only "certain companies" have available. This is an option that you, as a mortgage customer, can take advantage of.

A biweekly payment plan is simply a method of paying one-half of your normal mortgage payment every two weeks (biweekly) instead of paying a full payment monthly. By paying one-half of your monthly payment every two weeks (because there are fifty-two weeks in a year), you in essence make twenty-six half payments, or thirteen full payments, over the course of the year. This is a creative way to make one additional principal payment to your mortgage loan each year. If you decide to do this on your own, here are a couple of keys to the biweekly payment plan:

1. Initiate the process and make the payments on time. If you are going to do it on your own, you must notify your lender of your intentions and make sure that payments are being applied properly. If a lender offers to automatically deduct the payments from your checking account, be sure this is a free service, as many lenders or independent companies will charge for this service. Be sure to make payments on time to get the full benefit of the term reduction.

2. Make your first biweekly payment two weeks before the first payment is due. If you do not, choosing to wait until the first payment due date, you do not gain the full benefit of the principal reduction and could actually become delinquent on your payments because you only made a half payment on your due date and the other half two weeks later. Remember, the mortgage company expects a full payment *on* the first payment due date.

3. Pay *biweekly*, not *bimonthly*! This does not work if you make a half payment twice a month, because you are still only making twelve full payments. As a result, you do not get the benefit of the thirteenth payment. A bimonthly payment plan provides very minimal, if any, reduction in principal.

By paying biweekly, not only do you reduce the principal balance faster by applying one extra mortgage payment per year, but you also reduce the term significantly and reduce the *effective* interest rate. Why? Because by paying additional mortgage payments that reduce your principal and term faster than the terms you agreed to, you are in effect reducing the interest you will pay, which reduces the actual rate you pay on the loan (see chapter 2 for an explanation on rates).

The savings with a biweekly payment plan are significant. For example, on a $100,000 mortgage at 7.0 percent interest, you can shave seventy-five months from a thirty-year mortgage, paying off the balance in twenty-three years, nine months. In the process you'll pay $34,462 less in interest charges. For a fifteen-year $100,000 loan, you can pay off the balance almost two years quicker (thirteen years, one month). For a $250,000 loan at 6.0 percent, you would save $62,030 on a thirty-year mortgage and pay off the loan sixty-six months earlier. Similar savings appear on fifteen- and twenty-year mortgages.[2]

If you are planning to go through your lender or a third party to execute your biweekly plan, be sure it is a "true" bi-weekly payment arrangement. The key, once again, is paying a half payment every two weeks. This is a true biweekly plan and offers the greatest benefits for principal and term reduction. Many lenders, or third party providers, will offer biweekly plans but actually put the money into an account and apply the payments once a month. This is called a "standard," or pseudo, biweekly plan. Although you still receive substantial benefit, it is not to the same magnitude. For example, on the above $100,000 mortgage loan at 7 percent interest, making "standard" biweekly payments would save you $32,848 versus the $34,462 with the true biweekly plan. This is a difference of $1,614 in interest. Additionally, the term would be four months longer.

In order to set up a true biweekly payment plan, the lender must immediately credit each biweekly payment upon receipt and calculate the interest for the two-week interval. It is critical that you talk to your lender about the method by which they apply the payments in a biweekly plan to determine exactly what you are getting.

Strategy #2: Additional or Annual Payments

Another way to achieve nearly the same impact as a biweekly plan without the hassle is to apply one additional full payment to your mortgage on the same date each year. If you receive an annual bonus, this may be a good use for the money. Or, if you prefer, make 1/12 of an additional mortgage payment every month along with your normal mortgage payment. The key, in both cases, is to be sure to instruct the lender to apply the payments directly to principal. If you prefer, you could open a separate savings account that you put money into to build up to the full payment and then apply it at the end of the year. This way you earn interest on the funds while getting the benefit of the principal reduction. By doing this, the savings in interest and term are close to that of a true biweekly plan. That same $100,000 mortgage at 7.0 percent would save you $34,141 with additional one-twelfth payments. As a result, the term savings are nearly identical for the one-twelfth and the true biweekly mortgage payment plans.

According to Mortgage-x.com, your lender might offer several biweekly payment options, when you make a payment that equals half of your normal monthly payment every two weeks.[3] There is a considerable difference between payment plans, so you should check with the lender to find out exactly how they will treat your biweekly payments. There are also several Web sites that will provide free biweekly calculators so you can look at the impact of biweekly payments on your mortgage for yourself.

Strategy #3: Reverse Investment Philosophy

One last way to reduce your balance, term, payback, and effective interest rate is to apply the reverse investment philosophy. Simply put, this is where you make large lump sum payments on your mortgage. The benefits to doing this are substantial.

Why do we call it a reverse investment philosophy, or RIP? (It's not just because it allows you to "rest in peace"!) Instead of investing money into a fund that compounds interest, as we discussed in chapter 6, you are applying those monies toward your mortgage. What is the benefit? You actually receive a guaranteed investment return! Let's take a look at this:

Let's say that you have $50,000 that you receive through a bonus, inheritance, gift, etc., and you want to invest it. The traditional logic would be to invest it into some type of stock, bond, or money-market fund. You seek out advice from a financial expert and they ask you questions to determine your *risk tolerance.* Based on your risk tolerance, they recommend either an aggressive or conservative investment. The more aggressive, the greater the potential return and risk; the more conservative, the lower the potential return and risk. Although the projected return increases as you get more aggressive, the possibility of loss also increases. And by choosing to put the money in a very conservative or fixed-return investment with a probable return, you have to settle with the lowest return percentage. In addition, for both types of investments, you may have to pay a fee to the advisor to manage the fund, and you will have to pay taxes on the increases at some point in time. The bottom line is that there is a lot of potential, but also risk and expenses that can reduce the return on your investment.

Now, let's take that same $50,000 bonus or "inheritance" and see what happens if you apply it to your mortgage. By applying the entire amount, several things happen at the same time.

First, the mortgage balance drops immediately by $50,000 (less any interest due at payment). Because the lump sum is applied directly to your principal balance and no interest is charged on it, that means you pay 0 percent interest for that $50,000 portion of your balance. With a current interest rate of 6.5 percent fixed, you would save that 6.5 percent interest (less the adjustment for tax benefit) you would have paid on that money—guaranteed! That is why we call it a reverse investment: By not having to pay the 6.5 percent annual interest on the $50,000, the money you saved is equivalent to the interest you would have earned by investing that same $50,000 at the same 6.5 percent.

Remember, had you invested the $50,000, you would have been receiving whatever interest you earned, which is unknown and fluctuating depending on the investment and how it performs. At the same time you would have been making mortgage payments at a 6.5 percent rate that may have offset or wiped out the earnings. Although you don't earn income on the investment, you do avoid paying the interest at a fixed rate of 6.5 percent!

Second, by applying the $50,000 payment to the mortgage,

you accelerate the balance dramatically, reducing several years off of your mortgage term.

Finally, as you reduce the mortgage's term, you also reduce the long-term interest expense.

As for the tax ramifications to this, although you would lose the tax deduction benefits on your mortgage for that $50,000 portion of your balance, you may also avoid any potential capital gains or other taxes from the earnings on the investment. Before doing this, be sure to talk to a certified financial planner or investment professional and tax advisor to see a comparison of the actual after-tax savings for your situation.

NOTES

1. Assumptions used in determining personal payments were 2.5% payment calculation of outstanding balances for personal debt for the balance of $100,000, and 2.0% for the $250,000 balance. Actual percentages typically range between these estimates. For both mortgage balances, I assumed all refinances would be a twenty-five-year term and the rate would stay the same.

2. Information provided by Mortgage-X Mortgage Information Services (http://mortgage-x.com/calculators/biweekly_payments.asp)

3. Information from Mortgage-X (http://mortgage-x.com/library/biweekly .asp)

CHAPTER EIGHT

HOME EQUITY LOAN
Options

Throughout this book we have focused primarily on first mortgage financing. However, most of the benefits and principles we have discussed up to this point also apply to second mortgage financing, commonly referred to as home equity lending. A second mortgage loan is where we borrow against our equity, without affecting the first mortgage, to get cash for things like debt consolidation, home improvements, and other major life needs or to supplement a home purchase (as discussed in chapter 6).

Home equity lending includes both home equity loans and home equity lines of credit, or HELOCs. In some cases a second mortgage loan may actually be a better option for consolidating debt or accessing cash than a first mortgage refinance. The key is getting the right *kind* of second mortgage loan and configuring it in the most beneficial way.

Reasons to Consider a Home Equity Loan

Here are some of the determining factors that would dictate choosing a home equity loan or HELOC over a first mortgage refinance:

1. *A very low first mortgage interest rate.* Although rate is not the most important consideration in mortgage financing as we have discussed, it is certainly a significant one. In cases where your existing first mortgage is at an interest rate below the current market rates, choosing a home equity loan instead of refinancing can be a great choice.

2. *Short term remaining on first mortgage.* A home equity loan is also a great alternative when your existing first mortgage is nearly paid off and has a short term remaining, especially remaining terms less than ten years. Most first mortgage loan programs have a minimum term of ten years (many fifteen), but home equity loans can typically start at five years. Therefore, it would likely make more sense to leave your first mortgage intact, in order to not extend the term.

3. *Need for short-term cash.* If your need for the cash is short term, and you plan to pay it back quickly, a home equity loan or HELOC is a much better choice.

4. *Need for ongoing cash access.* HELOCs are an ideal tool for someone who needs access to cash on an ongoing basis, but has the financial wherewithal to pay it back in a timely fashion. In this case, the borrower has access to cash at any time and can pay it back quickly without having to pay additional loan fees other than the interest for the time they borrow the money.

5. *Need greater access to equity.* Many times, lenders will allow you to borrow against more of your equity in a home equity loan than they will in a first mortgage. As we discussed earlier, traditional first mortgage financing is 80 percent of your home's value with some higher loan

to value (LTV) programs going to 90 percent. However, some lenders will go up to 100 percent of your home's value in *combined* LTV, referred to as CLTV, on a home equity loan or HELOC. This depends completely on the loan amount, your qualifications, and the use of the money.

Ultimately, the best way to determine which is better for your situation, a home equity loan or first mortgage refinance, is to look at both and compare the benefits side by side to see which one provides the most monetary benefit for your situation.

Let's look back at the example used in the previous chapters to see the benefits and drawbacks had we chosen a home equity loan versus a first mortgage refinance. We will be looking at a fixed-rate, fixed-term second mortgage loan in this example, not a HELOC. (I will cover HELOCs in greater detail later in this chapter).

If you recall, the Jacksons refinanced their existing first mortgage of approximately $250,000 and accessed $75,000 additional cash for debt consolidation ($25,000) and investment ($50,000). What if, instead, they/we left the first mortgage alone and just borrowed the same $75,000 on a home equity loan? Let's look at a couple of different scenarios.

Category	Cash–Out Refinance	Home Equity Option 1 (20 Year Term)	Home Equity Option 2 (15 Year Term)
Mortgage amount	$325,000	$249,632	$249,632
Mortgage payment	$2,094 @ 6.0%	$1,697 @ 7.0%	$1,697 @ 7.0%
Term	25 Years	28 Years orig. mtg.	28 Years orig. mtg.
Home equity amount	N/A	$75,000	$75,000
Home equity payment	N/A	$518 @ 7.0%	$674 @ 7.0%
Total payments	$2,094	$2,215	$2,371
Payment difference	($228)	($107)	+ $49
Cash	$50,000	$50,000	$50,000
Total payback*	$584,100	$694,512	$691,512
Payback difference	N/A	$110,412	$107,412

*The personal debt payback was figured on a $625 payment for the $25,000 debt at an average rate of 13%.

What are the benefits of our using the twenty-year home equity option? The primary benefit is that the term for the additional $75,000 portion of the loan is five years less than the first mortgage. However, we lose $121 in payment reduction and three years term reduction on the existing first mortgage by doing so. As a result, there is actually an increase in the total payback of $110,412 over the first mortgage refinance.

As for the fifteen-year option, the term is reduced ten years for the $75,000, but the payments actually go up a little and, again, there is no reduction in the current first mortgage term.

The increase in payback, in comparison to the first mortgage refinance, is still substantially higher. As you can see, in these scenarios the first mortgage refinance is, by far, the better option.

Now let's refer back to the example of the Hunters with $186,116 in total debt to see a comparison between a home equity loan and first mortgage refinance. In this scenario we had $41,990 in personal debt we were paying off and twenty-seven years remaining on the current first mortgage.

Category	Cash Out Refinance	Home Equity Option 1 (20 Year Term)	Home Equity Option 2 (15 Year Term)
Mortgage amount	$186,116	$144,126	$144,126
Mortgage payment	$1,257 @ 6.5%	$899 @ 6.0%	$899 @ 6.0%
Term	25 Years	27 Years	27 Years
Personal debt	$0	$0	$0
Personal debt payments	$0	$0	$0
Home equity amount	N/A	$41,990	$41,990
Home equity payment	N/A	$325 @ 7.0%	$377 @ 7.0%
Total payments	$1,257	$1,224	$1,276
Payment difference	($745)	($778)	+ $19
Total payback	$374,100	$369,276	$359,136
Payback difference	N/A	($4,824)	($14,964)

In this case, the benefits of the twenty-year home equity loan (option 1) increase. Not only do we reduce the term for the $41,990 five years by not rolling it into the first mortgage, but the total payment reduction is $33 more. And even though we do not get the benefit of the two years' reduction in the current mortgage, the overall payback is less. Additionally, if we took the $33 in additional payment savings each month and applied it to the existing first mortgage, that mortgage would actually pay off in 24.8 years. Therefore, the twenty-year home equity option is a better option than the first mortgage refinance in this particular case.

As for the fifteen-year home equity loan (option 2), the payment is just a tad bit higher, but the $41,990 pays off ten years sooner than rolling it into the first mortgage and the payback is almost $15,000 less. In both cases, the home equity loan option would be the better approach.

Pros and Cons to Home Equity Lending

To determine the best type of mortgage for your personal situation, you have to compare the benefits of a first mortgage refinance and home equity loan. The benefits will speak for themselves.

Home equity loan advantages compared with mortgage refinancing: Because fees are usually charged as a percentage of the loan amount and the loan amounts are typically smaller, the fees for home equity loans and HELOCs are generally less than on a first mortgage finance. In addition, many times you can access more of your equity in a home equity loan than a first mortgage refinance. (Home equity can go up to a 100 percent combined LTV while first mortgages traditionally cap out at 90 percent.) Finally, home equity loans are typically for shorter terms and therefore may offer a better overall payback than first mortgage loans (depending on the remaining term of the existing first mortgage).

Home equity loan disadvantages compared with refinancing: Home equity loans are typically at a higher rate of interest than a first mortgage loan. In addition, you may lose the benefit of the existing first mortgage term reduction (unless you apply any additional payment savings on your own). Finally, the tax benefits of home equity loans are many times less than that of a first mortgage loan, simply because the lower balances mean lower taxes (and thus a much lower annual tax deduction).

Home Equity Lines of Credit (HELOCs)

Unlike the home equity loan, which has a fixed rate and term, home equity lines of credit, or HELOCs, fluctuate in both rate and term. I don't recommend using a HELOC for debt consolidation. Why? Because of the complexity of a HELOC and its unstable nature. A HELOC is a line of credit on your home. The lender establishes a maximum amount that you can borrow up to, based on your qualifications. You then have access to borrow money up to that amount, at your discretion, typically by writing checks.

The problem with using the line of credit for debt consolidation is that we might not be disciplined enough to control our spending habits and could end up accumulating additional debt and payments on our HELOC. The temptation to get deeper into debt can be too great. A line of credit on our house is like having access to a huge credit card—only every time we use it we eat away at our equity. And because we have access to so much cash instantly, the temptation for spending can become even greater. The Bible warns about the desire to have more: "If we have enough food and clothing, let us be content. But people who long to be rich fall into temptation and are trapped by many foolish and harmful desires that plunge them into ruin and destruction. For the love of money is the root of all kinds of evil."[1]

But there is even a bigger issue. HELOCs are based on fluctuating interest rates and terms. The rates change monthly or daily, thereby creating fluctuating payments. For example, you may have a HELOC where the monthly payments are based on a twenty-year amortization; therefore, every time you withdraw cash against your line of credit your balance increases and your payment adjusts to keep you on track for that term, raising your payment. In addition, some HELOCs have an initial term (for example ten years) with a balloon at the end. This means that whatever balance is left at the end of the initial ten-year term is due and payable in full. This may necessitate refinancing. If you do not qualify for refinancing at the time, you could literally be forced to sell your home.

Many HELOCs also offer a tempting interest-only option. In tough times, we tend to utilize this. If we do, we will pay nothing toward our principal to reduce our balance. That means you could pay for ten years and have the same balance as when you started. If your intent in consolidating debts is not just to reduce interest, reduce payments, and gain tax benefits but get out of debt, this is simply the wrong kind of loan to use to achieve that goal. A fixed-rate, fixed-term, short-term home equity loan is a much better choice.

So When Does a HELOC Make Sense?

As mentioned earlier, a HELOC makes great sense for the borrower who wants access to cash but is not a credit user *and* has the ability to pay it back quickly. A great example would be a self-employed individual. Let's say that you run a business and get large amounts of receivables in, but they are periodic and not consistent. You want access to cash in the low times but have the wherewithal to pay it right back when receivables come in. Instead of borrowing money up front, paying fees for the full amount borrowed, and then having to put it in an account that you can get to when you need it (which could end up costing you in taxes), you can get the money when you need it and pay interest *only* for the time you borrowed it. More important, with the HELOC, you can keep returning your balance to zero. And you still gain the potential tax benefits of a mortgage loan. The same advantages appear for someone who is gainfully employed, has good income, and needs to draw cash out, over time, for things like home improvements, but can pay it back quickly.

Home Equity Loans Can Be a Great Alternative

A home equity loan or a home equity line of credit may make a lot of sense in the right situation. The key, again, is to look at every option available, weigh the pros and cons, and choose what is best for your personal goals and situation.

NOTE

1. 1 Timothy 6:8–10.

CHAPTER NINE

TIPS FOR APPLYING FOR A
Mortgage

Now that you understand the roles of payment, cash, taxes, and term in choosing the right mortgage loan, it's time to find a mortgage loan. Here are critical tips for applying for a mortgage—from preparing for the mortgage transaction to comparing (shopping) rates to finding the right mortgage professional and company, as well as learning how to negotiate the best loan for your situation.

So the first step is to get on the phone or go online to "shop" or apply for a mortgage loan, right? Wrong. This would be a critical mistake because we are simply unprepared and unknowledge-able. This is the easiest way to get taken advantage of!

Preparing for a Mortgage Transaction

Most dread going through the mortgage application pro-cess. Why? We feel unequipped, overwhelmed, and vulnera-ble. Like anything in life, the key to changing this is knowledge and preparation. Before you ever contact a mortgage company, you can take several steps to prepare. These steps will help you to take control of the transaction by building your knowledge of your situation to ensure the absolute best deal.

With the right information about your situation, mortgage programs, and prevailing market rates, *you* will be in control of your mortgage and your financial future—not someone else! You also will make the loan officer's job much easier. The result: You get the best loan for your situation, there is little negotiation and headaches, and your loan closes much faster.

The Basics: Know Your Credit, Equity, and Income

To begin, you must know your basic qualifications. Four primary factors influence your loan eligibility; they are referred to in the mortgage business as the 4 Cs:

1. Collateral (property value and equity)
2. Capacity (income and debt)
3. Credit (pay history and credit score)
4. Character (overall stability)

Mortgage lenders use the first three as their primary criteria to determine loan eligibility. The fourth is used to determine an approval on a loan that may be marginal or tight on the first three. The key is to know the four Cs about yourself before you talk to a lender so that you already understand your qualifications and the type of loans you qualify for.

Collateral: Know Your Equity or Purchase Price

The equity position, or value of the property less liens or down payment, is the first and foremost qualifying criterion for a mortgage loan. The value and condition of the property is the main driver in establishing the availability of equity, or the *collateral*, to support the mortgage loan. To determine this, we need to establish the amount of equity we have to work with.

Determining Equity in a Mortgage Refinance

Determining your equity for a possible mortgage is a three-step process. First, determine *your home's current market value*. This is the value based on what homes are *selling* for, not *listing* for. The best method for determining this is to search recent sales of homes similar to yours in the area to determine your home's value. You can access this information through your local Realtors or on the Internet. If you have a recent appraisal, this may also be a good source. Using tax assessments, although a common practice, can be misleading because assessments are done only once per year at most. Therefore, depending on market appreciation or depreciation, these can be inaccurate. The value should be a *conservative*, not aggressive, estimate, as an appraisal done by a lender is usually more conservative than one done by a Realtor. The reason is to provide a value cushion.

Second, determine *the gross lendable equity*. Simply multiply the value by the highest loan-to-value (LTV) percentage you qualify for. This should be based on your income and credit (covered next). LTV is a percentage calculation that lenders use to determine the maximum amount they will lend on a property based on the borrower's qualifications. The better the qualifications, the higher the LTV, and the worse the qualifications, the lower. Typical LTVs for refinance transactions range from a high of 90 percent in today's market to a low of 70 percent, with 80 percent being standard. This means you may qualify for a loan anywhere up to 90 percent, depending on your qualifications and the loan program you choose. To get an idea of the LTV for your situation, simply go online and check the current lending guidelines based on your credit score and debt-to-income ratio.

Remember, the higher the LTV you accept on your loan, the higher the interest rate, fees, and costs are likely to be, but the more cash you have access to. In addition, when exceeding an 80 percent LTV, mortgage insurance will most likely apply and add additional costs to your mortgage loan.

Third, calculate *the net useable equity.* Subtract all mortgage balances and any other liens on your home[1] from the gross lendable equity calculated above to get the net useable equity. This amount represents the excess or shortage of lendable equity available. (In a first mortgage refinance, all liens must be paid off for the lender to be able to make the loan. In a second mortgage transaction, all liens except the first mortgage must be paid off.)

If the net lendable equity amount is less than the mortgage you desire, you will not qualify for a loan at this time. (If this is the case, be sure to read the next chapter, "What If I Don't Qualify?") If the total mortgage debt and liens on your home are less than the gross lendable equity, you may qualify. The difference represents the amount of equity you may be able to borrow against for debt consolidation or cash purposes. (See the chart "Determining Net Lendable Equity.") Here is a formula:

Property Value x LTV% = Gross Lendable Equity
Gross Lendable Equity = All Mortgage Balances and Liens
= Net Useable Equity

The chart "Determining Net Useable Equity" offers four examples with varying home values that show how mortgage balances and liens affect net useable equity. Notice that the first and last situations did not qualify for a mortgage loan unless the home values were higher or the LTV could be increased by the lender, because there simply was not enough value after all secured debts (mortgages and liens). However, in the second and third examples, each homeowner has ample equity to access additional cash to consolidate other debts, invest, etc.

Determining Net Useable Equity

Home Value x	Max LTV Qualifed for	= Gross Useable Equity	Less 1st Mtg. Balance	Less 2nd Mtg. Balance	Less Other Liens	= Net Useable Equity	Equity Qualifies?
$200,000	90%	$180K	$182K	$0	$0	($2,000)	No
$350,000	80%	$280K	$220K	$20K	$0	$40,000	Yes
$500,000	85%	$425K	$250K	$65K	$35K	$75,000	Yes
$125,000	80%	$100K	$65K	$0	$40K	($5,000)	No

Determining the Purchase Price in a Purchase Transaction

As discussed in chapter 5, determine the optimum purchase price and down payment amount based on your maximum affordable payment (MAP) and access to funds. Be sure that the mortgage loan amount (purchase price minus down payment plus any closing costs you want to include in the loan) does not exceed the LTV limitations of the loans out there. This is the amount you will use when applying for a mortgage used exclusively for a purchasing a home, known as a "purchase money mortgage."

Capacity: Know Your Income and Debt Ratio

Once you have determined that you qualify from an equity standpoint, you need to determine whether you qualify from an income-and-debt-ratio standpoint. Let's review how to calculate your DTI (debt-to-income) ratio. First, determine your total gross income by adding the *gross* (not net) income for all income sources you currently have. Divide that total by twelve, so you can know your monthly gross income. Be sure you can verify those income sources, as many lenders will not accept unverifiable income. Common forms of verification can include W-2s and tax forms, 1099s, recent year-to-date pay stubs, bank statements, and written verifications from employers or sources.

When you have totaled your gross income, divide that amount by the total debt payments you will have *after* the mortgage transaction. The result is your DTI. If your DTI exceeds 50 percent, you will not qualify in most cases. Standard DTIs range from 30 percent to 40 percent, depending on the lender. (See chapter 5 for recommended DTIs.) Although some lenders will approve loans up to 50 percent gross DTI, I caution against a mortgage loan when you have a DTI this high, unless you are in an extreme situation where you're at risk of losing your home and your payments are being reduced dramatically. In such a case, have a plan to sell the home afterward and buy something more affordable. If you are not in an extreme circumstance, work on reducing your debt on your own so you can be in a better position to qualify and afford the loan (see chapter 10).

Credit: Know Your Credit and Credit Score

Once you have determined whether you qualify from a collateral and capacity standpoint, it is time to determine if you qualify from a credit standpoint. Lenders rely heavily on credit payment history and credit scores to determine not just whether the borrower qualifies for a loan, but also the amount and price (the rate, points, and fees) they will offer on that loan. The better the payment history and the higher the credit score, typically the better the interest rate and the lower the fees and vice versa. The most common type of score used by lenders in the United States is a FICO score, a formula score developed by the Fair Isaac Corporation (or FICO). The FICO score ranges from 300 to 850; a score of 720 or higher usually has the best options for those seeking credit. BEACON scores are also commonly used, and each credit–reporting agency has its own credit score version.

In order to determine your payment history and credit score, as well as all debt reported on your credit report, you want to access your credit report before talking to a lender or mortgage professional. You can request a free credit report once a year from each of the three national credit reporting agencies (Trans-Union, Equifax, and Experian) at www.annualcreditreport .com. In fact, by rotating among the three agencies, you can get a free report every four months, a great way to keep up on your credit rating and monitor possible reporting errors by an agency. (The report is free. However, each agency will charge a nominal fee to release your FICO score.) Knowing your FICO and credit status not only helps you to understand if you will qualify and what kind of loan you qualify for, but also what kind of rate you can expect to pay and what kind of LTV you can get. Credit drives all three of these critical components of a loan. It is essential you know your credit history and credit score before you apply anywhere.

In addition to helping you understand what you qualify for,

knowing your credit score will give you a good idea of the rates that you should be getting charged.

Finally, be prepared with explanations of any delinquent credit, proof of paid debt, or legal actions and any other supporting documentation that shows that delinquent debt has been cured. This will help greatly in the application process and in the likelihood of getting approved.

Character: Understanding Your Credit Character

The last thing a lender will look at is your overall character as it pertains to a mortgage loan. This is based primarily on your stability. Things like length of residence and employment, stability of income, and use of debt all play a role in credit character. To best prepare for your loan application, have at least ten years of residence and employment, as well as explanations for residence or job changes, income changes, and recent debt.

Determine the Loan Amount, Term, and Purposes You Want

Once you determine you are a candidate for a mortgage loan, it is time to determine your loan amount and purpose. This is where you determine what *exactly* you want to apply for. Here are the factors you want to take into consideration:

1. *The loan amount.* First, based on your qualifications and the amount of cash you want, determine the loan amount you want to apply for. For a refinance, this means determining the maximum LTV you want based on your property value and the amount of cash you need. In a purchase, this means the amount you want to borrow and the

amount you want to put down (to determine your LTV). As discussed earlier, base your loan amount on your maximum affordable payment, or MAP. In both cases, this also means looking at what you can qualify for and afford based on your DTI *after the loan closes.*

2. *The term.* Determine what loan term you want based on your desired debt elimination date (see chapter 7).

3. *The purposes.* Finally, decide what you want to do with the cash. In a purchase this is a single purpose: buy your home. But in a refinance, this can be multiple purposes: debt consolidation, home improvement, investment, and so on. It is critical that you know exactly what you want to use the money for.

Determine Your Debt Payoff Amounts (for Debt Consolidation)

If your plan is to use any part of the cash from your refinance to eliminate debt, you need to determine the specific dollar amount needed to pay off those debts you plan to eliminate. In most cases, the payoff balances for your debts, particularly your mortgage loan, are different from what is reported on your credit report or on your monthly statements. The reason is that the payoff amount includes any additional interest accrued up to the date of payoff, any penalties, and any advances or additional charges (in the case of credit cards). In some cases it may be less if there are credits for interest rebates. To get the exact amounts, call your creditors to request your payoff balance for the date you anticipate the debts to be paid off. Be sure to ask for a per diem interest amount (daily interest calculation) so you know how much to add if the loan application takes longer than expected. Having this information will help you to know the total of your debts so you can determine if you have enough equity to pay them off, as well as to know how much excess equity you may have to access for cash. It also helps the mortgage company in moving through the process more quickly.

Know the Current Rates and Programs

Now you are ready to determine what rates and programs are available based on your qualifications and loan parameters; do this before speaking directly to a mortgage professional or applying for a loan. You can locate this information easily online. On the Internet you can find great Web sites that compare lender programs, rates, fees, etc., and also give you an idea of the going rates nationwide (such as www.bankrate.com). Do not waste lots of time trying to find the "lowest rate," as this is nearly impossible. As we discussed in chapter 2, the most competitive lenders are within an eighth to a quarter percent of each other. Finding *competitive* rates and fees is the key. Based on your findings, compute your monthly payment based on the rate, loan amount, and desired term so that you know exactly what the payment should be prior to talking to a mortgage professional. This will protect you from hidden fees. (There are several free online mortgage calculators out there you can access to do the calculations.) Then check that payment against your income to be sure you qualify from a debt-to-income (DTI) standpoint.

Who Can You Trust?

There has been much media attention in the past several years about dishonest and greedy mortgage companies and individuals. Frankly, in some cases these allegations were well founded. Improper and unethical business practices and, at times, fraud and pure dishonesty contributed to the "mortgage meltdown" of 2006 and beyond. All were shameful behaviors. It is important to remember, however, that not everyone was guilty. Those "bad apples" always are out there, but many great people serve in the mortgage business, and they really do try to do right by their customers. As borrowers, it is important that we find those people. It is also important that we challenge and test every loan officer to be sure they are out for our best interests, not theirs, and not just take them at their word.

Let me give you tips to do just that. After all, an honest mortgage professional who is truly out for your best interests and is providing the best loan for your situation would expect that and not be threatened or offended by it. Before I do that, here are a few cautions.

First, understand that mortgage loan officers are, by nature, salespeople. Their job is to "sell" you on their mortgage products, programs, rates, and company. Too often we rely on them to be the ultimate authority when it comes to choosing our mortgage loan. It is imperative that we do our homework and not just trust someone else's guidance or expertise with such a critical financial decision. This gives us ownership in our loan decisions, and it creates a good system of checks and balances.

The reason you want to be educated when entering into a mortgage transaction is that many in the industry are undertrained or inexperienced. Because there are no standard training requirements to be a loan officer (licensing is state, not federally, regulated and every state has different requirements), and every company has a different training philosophy, many loan officers never get formal training. Many learn on the job from their manager or colleagues, who may not have received formal training themselves. Even in those cases where they are trained, my experience has been that their training is mostly on the basics. Typically they are not experts on important issues like credit elimination and repair, tax, investments, financial planning, lending regulations, real estate, interest rates, and so on.

Second, the mortgage industry has a high level of employee turnover, so you may be working with someone who is new to the business and still trying to learn the fundamentals. Therefore, the mortgage originator you work with may not be well trained, if trained at all, and not have a full working knowledge of mortgages and all of the particulars surrounding mortgage transactions and the mortgage industry.

Third, while some mortgage originators are paid a salary, some earn a salary plus commission and others receive a straight commission. Those who do work on commission may earn their commission as a flat fee or as a percentage of the fees earned on the loan. In this case, they have a vested interest in the loan. It is important to find out how your loan officer gets paid. But keep in mind, paying a little more to the loan officer does not necessarily mean they are a bad choice. It all depends on what they are providing. For example, if you get a loan officer who is commissioned but really spends a lot of time understanding your financial goals and finding the very best program available for your situation, and he or she offers you a loan with much greater benefits to you than the competition's, that loan officer may end up ultimately saving you more money even after the higher commission.

It all comes down to who ultimately provides you the best *overall* mortgage and savings (what I will define later as net tangible benefit)! Remember, the loan officer can serve a great role if they do their job well, and in doing so, should get paid, too! When a loan officer really does offer you the best loan for your situation, one that changes your life, they have earned their commission. But always remember: no one is more interested in your best interest than you; therefore, you must prepare yourself and enter into a mortgage with knowledge and confidence so you can have the control!

Finding a Reputable Mortgage Provider

Now that you understand a little more about the person you are working with, the most important step begins: finding that honest, reputable, and competitive mortgage professional and mortgage company to work with. For starters, I recommend interviewing at least four companies. You will want to be able to compare offers among different companies to ensure the best deal and to create competition.

Whenever possible, start with someone you have worked with in the past, provided that you were happy with their service. If this is your first mortgage transaction, or you have not worked with someone in the past whom you would use again, look for a referral from someone you know and trust who has had a great experience. If neither of these apply, start with your local bank and the most competitive companies on the Internet.

Whatever the case, it is critical that you never talk with just one company or mortgage professional, no matter how long you have known them or no matter how highly they come referred. We tend to go back to companies we have used in the past, simply because we are comfortable with them. Although there is great value in working with someone you know and have had experience with, you still want to be sure they are giving you the best deal possible. It is your money and your mortgage! Therefore, always get *at least* one comparison, preferaby three, when using a previous source or referral to keep that person honest and competitive. This creates a great system of accountability for that person and ensures you the best deal for you and your family. If they are looking out for your best interest, they will not be offended by you talking to another company, but will take it as an opportunity to prove their worth. You may even end up getting a little better price out of them at the end of the day.

One additional note—I recommend you investigate and compare mortgage providers on your own. Do not rely on lender aggregate companies (these are companies that supply offers from four different lenders) as your sole source. Such a company can be one of the four sources you inquire with, but it should not be the only source. Remember these companies are simply referring mortgage providers that have signed up with their network and paid to utilize their marketing. Unless they can give you a guarantee of the best mortgage provider, this does not ensure you are getting the most competitive mortgage providers.

Mortgage Brokers, Mortgage Bankers, and Mortgage Lenders

Let's look at the three most common forms of mortgage providers out there and the differences among them: mortgage brokers, mortgage bankers, and mortgage lenders. A mortgage broker is an individual or company who works independently, not for any specific lender, and *refers* loan applications to several different lenders. Their role is to place you with a mortgage lender suited to your qualifications and loan criteria. The broker is a liason between you and the lender.

Like mortgage brokers, mortgage bankers have access to several lenders; however, they can actually fund your loan themselves and then sell it to the lender after it is closed. Because of this, they may be able to offer a little better loan pricing.

Mortgage lenders (which includes independent mortgage companies, banks, savings and loans, credit unions, and such governmental agencies as Fannie Mae, Freddie Mac, and the Federal Housing Adminstration) offer specific mortgage programs that they have developed internally. There are advantages and disadvantages to each.

The advantage of a mortgage broker or banker with their access to multiple lender programs is that they are not as limited in the mortgage products they can place you in compared to the mortgage lender who can offer only its own lending programs. As a result, *if they are doing their job correctly*, a mortgage broker or banker can be a great resource for finding the best mortgage programs for your situation.

However, because the mortgage broker or banker is independent, there can be additional fees charged that you would not have to pay if you went directly to the mortgage lender. In some cases, these fees are paid by the lender directly. In other cases, the broker charges you directly. If you prefer to have someone work on your behalf to find you a loan and do not want to do the work yourself, a mortgage broker or banker can be a great choice. Although you may pay a little more in fees, if the broker or banker truly finds you the best program, even after the premium, it may be worthwhile using them, as their knowledge and experience helped you find that program you may not have found on your own.

However, if you prefer to do the work on your own, which is easier today because of the Internet, you may save yourself some money by going directly to a mortgage lender. Understand, however, there is no cut-and-dried rule of thumb. You may find a better rate through a broker or banker than you would with a direct lender. The choice—lender, broker, or banker—is yours!

Tips for Choosing a Mortgage Provider

The key to choosing the right mortgage provider is to talk with each one, know every cost associated with their loan program, and compare the different offers to determine who is providing the most competitive and beneficial loan for your situation.

To achieve this, I would recommend that of the four companies you compare, include at least one broker, one banker, and one lender. Let them compete to provide you with the best loan for your situation and *earn* your business. The goal is to ultimately get the best deal. Keep in mind that in many cases the rate and fees originally quoted are negotiable. By working with different companies and comparing among them, you can get them to offer their best rate and program to get your business.

But remember, as we have discussed throughout this book, the lowest rate does not necessarily mean the best loan. Although you certainly always want to get the best possible rate for the program you choose, ultimately to determine the best loan you want to compare loan offers based on the payment, cash availability, tax benefits, and term.

Here are six initial tips for evaluating and choosing a mortgage provider:

1. Be sure the company is licensed (if required by state).
2. Ask for testimonials that you can verify yourself by phone.
3. Evaluate the company's experience and knowledge.
4. Look for experience, credentials, certifications, training, etc., in the individual you are considering.
5. Request written letters of endorsement that you can check for authenticity.
6. Investigate the individual or company for credibility (number of years in business, number of employees, Web site, annual reports, online search for negative postings, Better Business Bureau, state regulatory authority, etc.).

Working with Potential Mortgage Providers

When shopping for a mortgage loan, there are several questions you want to ask of any mortgage provider. First, you want to communicate your qualification information so that the person you are dealing with can quote you an up-front program. So the mortgage representative can quote you his or her best rate and program, have these items available when applying:

1. Property value and justification for value (comparable sales, recent appraisals, etc.) and purchase price of home

2. All mortgage and debt statement payoff balances, and down payment amount

3. Desired loan amount and specific purposes for funds (including debts and reasons for paying off)

4. Credit score from recent credit report and explanation for any and all delinquency for past ten years (including bankruptcies, legal actions, and past due credit)

5. Annual and recent gross income documentation (including W-2s, 1099s, pay stubs, tax forms, rental receipts, bank statements, and any other proof of income)

6. After-loan DTI calculation based on loan amount you are applying for at estimated current interest rates

7. Last ten years' residence and employment information

By being prepared with this information, the mortgage company has what it needs to provide you an initial quote. Although you will not be able to get the final quote until you have completed the application process, this gives you a starting point to select the company you want to move forward with to the application process. Being prepared with this information will not only impress the mortgage professional and make their job easier, but it allows you to step into the application and rate negotiation process with confidence and control!

Questions for Your Lender

Here are a series of standard questions you want to ask every mortgage professional you work with about their products and programs when shopping for a mortgage loan. This will tell you what they are providing based on your needs and qualifications:

Questions on Loan-to-Value, Down Payment, and Term

You want to understand the maximum LTV programs available, based on your qualifications, to be sure that you know your options for maximizing cash (refinance) or minimizing your down payment (purchase). Questions on down payment and term will help you get the answer. Here are four key questions:

1. What is the maximum LTV available based on my qualifications (for refinances or purchases)?
2. What is the minimum down payment required based on my qualifications (for purchases only)?
3. In addition to thirty- and fifteen-year terms, do you also have ten-, twenty-, and twenty-five-year loan terms?
4. Do you have both fixed- and adjustable-rate programs available?

The purpose of these questions is to determine if the mortgage provider has access to the mortgage programs that you desire for cash, term, and program availability. If they do not have what you are looking for, move on to the next company and do not spend any more time. If they do, move to the next set of questions.

Questions on Interest Rate and APR

Next, based on the LTV option you choose and your overall qualifications (property value or equity, income, DTI, and credit), you want to establish the best interest rate they have available. To find out the true costs, be sure to ask questions about the interest rate and APR separately. (I will discuss questions on fees later.) This helps you determine if the fees are financed in the loan. If the interest rate and APR are the same, then there are either no fees (unlikely), the fees are paid completely up front, out-of-pocket, or the fees are paid directly to the mortgage originator by the lender (which will typically increase the interest rate). Note the last question; this is an accountability question to ensure complete honesty.

1. What is the lowest fixed-interest rate available based on my credit score, overall qualifications, and the loan program I am looking for? What is the APR for that same loan?
2. What is the lowest adjustable rate mortgage loan based on that same loan? What is the APR?
3. Can you provide that to me in writing?

Remember, by law your mortgage provider has to disclose to you every fee they are charging on your loan in the Good Faith Estimate (GFE). However, the GFE is only an estimate. The actual fees can change by the time the loan closes. Be sure to recheck all fees again, in writing, prior to closing.

Additional Questions for Adjustable Rate Mortgages (ARMs)

If an adjustable rate mortgage is what you are looking for, be sure to ask these additional questions to completely understand all aspects of the ARMs being offered.

1. *What is the initial term, or reset date, of the ARM?* In most cases, adjustable rate mortgage loans have an initial term where the rate does not change. For a first mortgage

this is typically three, five, or seven years (for example, a 5/25 has a five-year fixed-rate initial term, with a twenty-five-year remaining term that adjusts annually or semi-annually. A 5/1 ARM has a five-year fixed-rate initial term and then adjusts annually every year thereafter). The rate "resets" at the end of the initial period to current market conditions at the time. After the initial reset, ARMs can adjust, or reset, at a specified date for the remainder of the loan term (usually annually). HELOCs typically do not have an initial fixed term. The rates on these products typically change daily or monthly.

2. *When and how often does the rate adjust after the initial term?* As mentioned, ARMs have rate adjustment periods after the initial term. You need to know the frequency of these future adjustments to be aware of when and how often the rate and payment can potentially change after the initial term.

3. *What is the maximum rate adjustment (referred to as the rate cap) for each adjustment period?* Adjustable rate mortgages typically have an interest rate cap each time they adjust or "reset." A common cap is 2 percent. This means that at the adjustment period, the rate can increase by a maximum of 2 percent. This is critical information to know so that you can determine the maximum your payment can go up to at the time of each reset.

4. *What is the maximum lifetime interest rate adjustment, or the fully indexed rate?* The lifetime cap, or fully indexed rate, is the maximum amount the rate can increase by during the life of the loan. A common lifetime cap is 7 percent. Therefore, if you have a loan that starts at prime

plus 2 percent, it can go as high as prime plus 9 percent. (For example if you started with a 7 percent rate, that could take your rate to as high as 14 percent! This is why adjustable rate mortgages can be so dangerous.)

5. *What is the minimum interest rate for each adjustment period and the life of the loan?* Most ARMs also have what's called a floor rate. This is the lowest the rate can ever be. Although ARMs have large rate caps that allow for a substantial risk to the borrower in an increasing rate market, they have small rate floors allowing for very little benefit in a decreasing rate market. Many lenders establish a floor rate of one–half percent below the start rate (the initial rate of the loan). Therefore, even if rates drop 2 percent, the rate on the loan will only drop .5 percent. The lender gains the benefit of the market in this situation, not the borrower.

6. *What is the index that the rate is tied to?* The interest rate will be determined by moves in a particular index. Common indexes include the prime lending rate as reported by the *Wall Street Journal*'s bank survey ("Prime"), 11th District cost of funds index ("COFI"), Treasury bills ("T-bills"), and the London Inter Bank Offer Rate ("LIBOR"). Depending on the market at the time, there can be clear advantages to you as the borrower in choosing one index over another.

7. *What is the margin?* The margin is the amount of interest paid over the index. For example, a loan quoted as "prime plus 2 percent" is an adjustable rate loan where the prime lending rate is the index and 2 percent is the margin. If the prime lending rate was 5 percent and the

margin was 2 percent, then the current interest rate would be 7 percent.

Questions on Loan Fees and Costs

Once you understand the rate, the APR, and the parameters of the ARM you may be considering, you must be able to recognize any fees associated with the loan. Remember, many fees are separate from the interest rate and APR. Your goal is to know every single fee and cost associated with the loan, and whether it is paid up front and out-of-pocket or financed in the loan. This will help you get a picture of the true cost of the loan, so when you compare offers between lenders, you are not just comparing on rate, but actual cost.

Here are a dozen questions that will help you spot and evaluate the various fees and how they will be paid:

1. What are *all* the loan and origination fees for the loan, including front and back end or any discount points (fees paid to a lender at closing in order to lower your interest rate)? Each discount point is equal to 1 percent of the loan amount, but it lowers the interest rate. For example, each discount point paid on a thirty-year loan typically lowers the interest rate by approximately 0.125 percent.
2. Are there any fees that you, as the mortgage originator, will earn directly from the lender that are not disclosed in the loan documents? (These fees are the YSPs, or yield spread premiums, mentioned briefly in chapter 1.)
3. Of the fees being charged, which are financed in the loan and which do you have to pay up-front, out-of-pocket?
4. Are there any additional "junk" fees (processing, under-

writing, closing) being charged that you haven't yet been told about?

5. Are these fees financed in the loan or paid up front?
6. Is there an appraisal fee and who pays it?
7. Is the appraisal paid up front or financed in the loan?
8. Is there mortgage insurance required on the loan?
9. What is the amount of the mortgage insurance (if applicable)?
10. Is the mortgage insurance included in the loan payments, paid up front, or paid by the lender?
11. Are there any prepayment penalties on the loan?
12. If so, when do they occur and how much are they?

Some companies have actually moved to fixed fees on their loans like many car dealers have done. This is a good alternative provided the fees are competitive. Make your mortgage company disclose to you every fee they are charging on your loan, no matter how small!

Questions on Loan Programs

The next step is to get the specifics of the loan program itself to start to determine the actual loan being provided.

1. Is this a fully amortized loan (a fully amortized loan is one where the payments over the term pay the loan in full)?
2. Are there any balloons? (A balloon is an amount due at the end of the regular term. This is found in some HE-LOCs, where there is an initial term, typically five or ten years, with the balance due at the end.)

3. Is there any other creative financing to this loan that needs to be known that has not already been mentioned, such as negative amortization where the balance goes up initially?
4. Are biweekly payment plan options offered?
5. If so, what is the availability and cost?

Final Questions

Now you want to sum up all of this with the key questions that will determine the exact loan you will be getting.

1. Based on everything discussed, what is the final loan amount and amount financed (chapter 2)?
2. What is the final rate and APR?
3. What is the term of the loan and the ending payment date?
4. Based on the term requested, what is the exact monthly payment for the loan?
5. Is this a fully amortized principal and interest payment?
6. Does it have an interest-only option or component?
7. Could you please break down where all of the money is going?
8. If I decide to move forward, can you provide that itemization, including costs and fees, in writing today?

Keep Them Honest

Once you get the quotes, calculate the loan parameters to make sure that everything you were told was truthful. Remember, there are only four calculations to a mortgage loan: the rate, the payment, the loan amount, and the term. Entering any three in a mortgage calculator will calculate the fourth. Therefore, to be sure the information is accurate, simply calculate to make sure the numbers all match up. If in calculating you find that the numbers do not match up, contact the loan officer to find out why. If he or she lied to you, eliminate that candidate. You never want to deal with someone who is dishonest.

Part of keeping them honest is to get all offers and specific figures in writing. As mentioned earlier, once you have completed the application process, the mortgage company, by law, must provide a Good Faith Estimate (GFE) within three business days. The estimate must include an itemized list of fees and costs associated with your loan. These fees, also called settlement costs or closing costs, cover every expense associated with the mortgage loan, including inspections, title insurance, taxes, and other charges. The key here is that it is an estimate. Because the GFE is provided before the income is verified, appraisals are completed, and title is done, the numbers quoted are not the actual numbers you will see on your final loan documents; in many cases they will change.

Remember to get all offers in writing. Request a written form that outlines everything you are being offered before making any decision.

Compare the Quotes

Once you have spoken to four mortgage providers and have four quotes that are accurate, the final step is to compare the quotes to find the best. Again, the best is not necessarily the lowest rate, but the one that provides the best terms, with the best benefits, at the best rate and fees overall. Once you have found the two best of the four offers, it is time to investigate those companies to be sure they are reputable and then submit your application.

Finally, if the loan is a mortgage refinance, go beyond the costs and benefits and be sure that the loan has net tangible monetary benefit, or NTMB. This is a concept I touched on earlier and is one of the most important steps in ensuring you are getting a loan that *really benefits you!* The method to determine NTMB is very simple. Take the *costs of the loan* for the period of time you expect the loan to be open and compare them to the monetary benefits of the loan for that same period. (You do this by adding up any payment reduction, cash-out, tax savings, and deferral benefits for the period of time you chose.) I recommend using at minimum a one-year comparison. If the total loan costs and fees are less than the monetary benefits for the period of time used, there is a short-term net tangible monetary benefit. If, in addition, you reduce your mortgage term, the loan also provides a long-term benefit.

To compare the NTMB of loan offers between two companies, you can do the same for each of the loans and then compare them against each other to see which one provides you with the most NTMB.

One final note. Many times the reason we end up with a bad loan is because we are in a rush to close the loan. Although I understand that sometimes circumstances dictate this, whenever possible, take your time. Do not be in a hurry! This is the biggest and longest financial decision you may ever make; you don't want to rush it. Take your time; negotiate the best deal with the best company so you get a loan you can really live with.

Don't Be Afraid to Negotiate

Most loan rates and fees are negotiable. Never be afraid to negotiate with your mortgage provider. Use comparative offers to get companies to work against each other. But remember, someone can quote you anything right up to the point of closing and then change the fees and costs at closing. So don't go with someone because they say they are the lowest. Go with the company that is competitive, provides the most benefit, and is honest, relational, interested in your well-being, and responsive to your needs. Price is not everything—trust is! You want to get a great rate on a great loan, but you also want to get it from a great mortgage professional. Be wary of the loan officers who can "beat anyone" and always make it about rate!

Don't Be Afraid to Walk Away

As in any buying situation, the one who is willing to walk away usually gets the best deal. Millions of borrowers have gone through the mortgage application process, only to find out that the loan was different at closing. Unfortunately, many of those same borrowers stayed with the deal anyway because they were so close to getting the money. Remember that in a refinance, once you sign your loan you have a minimum three-business-day rescission period (not including Sunday or holidays) to review your loan documents and cancel if the loan terms have changed in any way. In a purchase, you can request prior to closing that the documents be reviewed by you and your attorney. Don't ever hesitate to take this option if you have been misled. Even though you will have to go through the process again with another company, you will have lots of knowledge and information that will expedite the loan. The last thing you ever want to do is take a loan that will really harm you in the long run to save a little time in the short run. Moreover, you never want to reward dishonest behavior by buying.

Don't Be Afraid to Go to the Top

If you feel you have been misled or deceived by someone, go straight to the management of that company—all the way to the president, if necessary. In most cases, the management team wants to know and can do something to fix it. A dishonest loan officer does not make a dishonest mortgage company. Although there are some dishonest companies out there, most try to do it right. All it takes is one greedy or dishonest individual to taint that. Most companies do not want people representing them dishonestly any more than you want to work with a dishonest individual. By letting them know, you help them and yourself.

Final Tips for Getting the Best Loan

Here are seven final tips for financing (or refinancing) your mortgage:

1. Always lean toward fixed-rate, fixed-term financing. The only exception is when you have a lower rate ARM option where the initial term, or reset date, is after you will be out of the house (for example in a case where you know you are moving in two years due to a job relocation and you are getting a five-year initial term on your ARM). Be absolutely certain you will be out of the home before the end of the initial ARM adjustment period! Because noth-

ing is certain, lean toward fixed-rate, fixed-term whenever possible.

2. Always get a fixed-rate loan in an environment where rates are volatile and trending upwards.

3. Be wary of claims for "no cost loans." There are usually fees on the loan somewhere—they may just be hidden. Remember, the mortgage company is in business to make money; they do not work for free.

4. Always lean toward shorter term financing. When refinancing, it is especially important to reduce your term, if at all possible, even if it takes sacrifice. Consider a twenty-five or twenty- or fifteen-year mortgage instead of the traditional thirty years. In addition to saving you thousands in interest and paying off sooner, you will usually get a lower interest rate on a shorter term loan.

5. Avoid a prepayment penalty clause in your loan whenever possible, unless you are certain you will not pay off the loan before the prepay period ends and can gain a premium priced loan as a result. There is no standard requirement for prepayment penalties.

6. Remember, what you ultimately pay and get are based on all of the parameters of the loan. Do not make a decision based on just a minor rate difference or a little higher fee, but on the actual benefits of the loan. Compare payment, cash, tax, and term benefits between different companies and choose the loan that ultimately gives you the most.

7. Get out of debt as soon as possible!

8. If you know, based on your research, that you qualify for a prime rate, do not allow anyone talk you into a higher interest rate. Don't be bullied; be confident! Preparation

gives you the advantage. Do not trust anyone who contradicts your analysis.

Seeking a new mortgage armed with knowledge and preparation raises the probability that you will have a mortgage loan that meets your needs both in the short and long term.

NOTE

1. This includes your first mortgage, any additional mortgages or home equity loans or lines of credit, plus any liens (such as an IRS tax lien).

WHAT IF I DON'T
Qualify?

I f you who have read this far and have debt you want to eliminate but, after reviewing the guidelines, have determined
that you do not have the equity or income to qualify for a
mortgage, here's help. This chapter will address specific steps
you can take to improve your financial situation, eliminate your
debt, and position you for future mortgage opportunities.

Determine Your Total Monthly Outgo

The first step is to determine your total financial situation and budget, beginning with totaling your mortgage and
personal debt amounts and payments. (If you have not yet
done this, you can access tools to help you on our Web site
at www. mortgagepowered.com.) Next, document and add
every additional expense (non-debt) you currently have to
establish your *total outgo*. This includes living expenses like
food, utilities, clothing, and gas, as well as charitable giving,
entertainment, and miscellaneous expenses. You can do this
yourself on a simple piece of paper or Excel spreadsheet, or
access any of a number of budgeting tools online.

Every single monthly expense needs to be accounted for so
that you know where your money is going. Be sure to include
a category for cash expenses. The best way to do this is to use a

debit card for as many of your purchases as possible to keep a record of all cash expenses.

Identify Your Shortage or Excess

Once you have your monthly outgo accounted for, subtract that amount from your total *net* monthly income (after taxes). This step will determine your *spendable income.* If your monthly outgo is more than your income, you have a *shortage.* If your outgo is less than your income, you have an excess.

Review, Reduce, and Remove

Whether you have a shortage or excess, you will want to take time to review, reduce, and remove the non-debt expenses. This third step will help you create more spendable income to use toward eliminating your debt. By analyzing all of your expenses, you can determine which ones are unchangeable and which ones can be altered. Immediately remove those expenses which are unnecessary. Once completed, determine what remaining expenses you can reduce. Come up with a feasible, yet aggressive, reduction amount that you can manage your budget with. In essence, you are creating a new budget to live by. You will now be in a position to use the money you freed up to eliminate your debt.

Personal Debt Elimination System (PDES)

Now that you have improved your expenses and created additional spendable income, you can start moving toward debt elimination. From the excess spendable income you established in the previous step, determine the *maximum amount you can apply to your debt to eliminate it in the shortest time possible.*

We will refer to this as your Debt Elimination Investment (DEI). Once you have determined your DEI, you are going to use this to initiate your Personal Debt Elimination System (PDES). The process is really very simple; it is modeled after a common debt elimination process referred to as "snowballing," but utilizes DPR percentages to accelerate the elimination of the debt even faster. The way snowballing works is this: You build up (snowball) the amount you pay on your *personal* debt each month, eliminating your debts *one at a time*, by applying additional payments to your lowest balance *personal* debt until that debt is paid off. Once paid off, the payment you were making on that debt is then added to the next smallest debt, including the additional payment, to accelerate the payoff on that debt, and so on and so on. You continue this method of *snowballing* your payments until your debt is completely eliminated.

By altering this formula to focus on debt-to-payment relationship, we can actually increase the payoff of the debt even faster. Instead of starting with your smallest debt and working to the highest, start with the personal debt that has the *highest* DPR and work to the *lowest* DPR. The higher the percentage of payment to debt, the more you are gaining in both balance and interest reduction. See the charts at the end of this segment (pages 203, 204) for an example of the impact from this debt elimination process and a comparison to the traditional snowball method.

Requirements for Success Using the PDES

Here are three requirements for success with this personal debt elimination system:

1. *Start with and maintain the maximum debt elimination investment.* Start with the maximum investment you can afford, then continue to pay that amount until the debt is gone. As you see the debts begin to drop, you may be tempted to reduce the amount you are paying. Resist the temptation! If you do so you will dramatically extend the time frame of the debt elimination.

2. *Do not add to or reopen the debts.* If you use your credit cards during the elimination process, you will wipe out any gains you will have made. In addition, once the debts are eliminated, do not reopen them. With credit cards, in particular, you must apply great discipline here. Understand that as you pay down and pay off credit card debt, your creditor may increase your line of credit because of your good pay history, creating the potential for even more debt. When you eliminate a credit card, shred the card and send a letter to the creditor asking them to close the account and take you off their mailing list. Also, subscribe to the national "do not call" list and request that your name be removed from third-party mailing lists they may sell. This will remove the temptation to get back into debt.

3. *Stick to your budget.* Remember, your goal is to eliminate your debt. Stick to the budget you have established so you can stay on track for debt elimination.

Mortgage Debt Acceleration Program

As soon as you have eliminated the personal debt, apply the same payment amount you were making to the personal debt to your mortgage balance. Continue making the excess payment until your mortgage is paid off.

Let's look at what happens if we apply the steps we just learned by using the example of the Hunters, whose debts included two car loans and various credit cards. After developing a budget, the Hunters determine that they have $200 in additional spendable income that can be applied as the Debt Elimination Investment (DEI). If we are the Hunters, we first must establish the DPR for each debt by dividing the payments by the debt. Then, based on the DPR, we rank the debts to determine the order of payoff. If we have two debts with the same DPR, always pay off the smaller balance first:

Personal Debt	Int. Rate	Current Paymt.	Current Balance	DPR%	Ranking
Car loan	5.5%	$477	$20,533	2.3%	6
Car loan	6.0%	$328	$10,803	3%	3
MC	7.0%	$133	$5,318	2.5%	5
Visa	13.25%	$81	$3,247	2.5%	4
Dept. store	23%	$35	$875	4%	1
Dept. store	23%	$49	$1,214	4%	2

The next chart shows the personal debts ordered by their ranking. If we start the process of debt acceleration by applying the $200 DEI to the first debt and increasing each time, notice what happens to the payoff schedule:

Rank	Personal Debt	Rem. Term	Starting Balance	Required Payment	DEI	Adjusted Payment	Paid Off
1	Dept. store	2.9 Yrs	$875	$35	$200	$235	3.8 mos.
2	Dept. store	2.8 Yrs	$1,214	$49	$235	$284	7.9 mos.
3	Car loan	3 Yrs	$10,803	$328	$284	$612	22.5 mos.
4	Visa	4.5 Yrs	$3,247	$81	$612	$693	25.8 mos.
5	MC	3.8 Yrs	$5,318	$133	$693	$826	29 mos.
6	Car loan	4 Yrs	$20,533	$477	$826	$1,303	34.2 mos.
All Personal Debt Paid Off At:							34.2 mos.
7	Mortgage	27 Yrs	$144K	$899	$1,303	$2,202	6.25 yrs.
Debt Free							9.10 yrs.

Personal Debt Elimination

As you can see, by using this method, and only raising the payments $200 per month, all of the personal debt is paid off in 34.2 months—less than three years! The average term of the debt was 3.5 years when we started, but this was based on the cards never being used, the rate never changing, and the payments staying the same. Again, the likelihood of this is minimal. Therefore, in a worst-case scenario, the Hunters reduced their debt by almost eight months. At $1,103 in original payments, that is $8,824 in payment savings. When you offset the $200 DEI for the 34.2 months, the savings is still $1,984.

Mortgage Debt Elimination

If the Hunters could afford it, by continuing to apply the $1,303 in personal debt payments to the mortgage for the next 6.25 years, they would completely eliminate their mortgage debt in 9.1 years. In other words, their mortgage term reduces from twenty-seven years to about nine! This is an eighteen-year reduction, or 65 percent, in the term. By simply multiplying the monthly payments of $899 by the eighteen-year reduction, you can see that the gross savings in payments is $194,184! When you offset the $1,303 in payments applied for the 6.25 years it took to pay off the mortgage in 9.5 years (a total of $97,725), there is a net savings in payments of $86,459.

If the Hunters decided they didn't want to apply all $1,303 in payments they were making after the personal debt was eliminated to improve their spendable income, but still wanted to pay off their mortgage sooner, they could do so by simply determining their desired mortgage debt elimination date (as we covered in chapter 7) and paying the additional amount needed to get there. For example, if they wanted to pay off the 24 years 2 months they had remaining after eliminating the personal debts in 15 years, they would only have to pay an additional $257 per month ($622 to pay off in 10 years). With their personal debt gone, they now have a lot more options for financial freedom!

Developing a New Budget

I believe everyone, regardless of income or excess, should develop a budget. In today's volatile economy and uncertain times, we should be good stewards of all that we have been given. A Bible verse articulates this truth: "Be careful how you live. Don't live like fools, but like those who are wise. Make the most of every opportunity in these evil days."[1]

No matter how much we make today, and how much security we feel we have, one major shift in the economy, our employment, or our health could change all of that in the blink of an eye. Therefore, we should be wise with our money now. Anything we save can be used as additional resource should something happen later. By budgeting, we can find areas where we can reduce expenses and take the money to use for major life expenses like college or retirement, or donate to a great cause.

Because our primary focus in this book is on mortgages and financial freedom, I don't want to spend a lot of time on teaching you the entire process of developing a budget. There are many great books and resources that have already done that. My favorite resource is Crown Financial Ministries (www. crown.org). Howard Dayton, a long-time author and executive at Crown Financial Ministries, wrote a bestselling book titled *Your Money Map*. I would recommend you invest in that book. It will provide you with great tips on money, budgeting, and finances, but will also give you the biblical foundation for every principle. If you prefer to check out other budgeting and financial resources, we have put a listing on our Web site—www. mortgagempowered.com.

Tips for Those with Severe Mortgage Delinquency or Foreclosure

You may be one of the millions of unfortunate individuals affected by the severe housing market conditions of 2007 through early 2009. Perhaps you faced late payments on your mortgage, maybe even foreclosure. If that has happened to you, let me say how sorry I am that you have encountered such challenges. Although I cannot address every option available to you, because the programs and options are changing all the time, I want to provide you with some basic tips. I would also recommend visiting our Web site at www.mortgagempowered .com for the most recent list of suggested mortgage program alternatives.

Reduce Expenses or Increase Income

The first option you want to consider, and the most optimum, is to reduce your expenses (as covered earlier) to create an opportunity to afford the loan and make up the past due payments. In addition, you may want to consider taking on a second job to supplement your income.

Sell

If you cannot afford the home, the next best option is to sell the property on your own and recover any profit remaining from the equity. The key here is to work with your lender during the sales process to try and come up with a plan to keep the mortgage current and maintain good credit.

Contact Your Lender

Reports have shown that most borrowers, when in trouble on their mortgage, avoid talking to their lender. The reason cited is that the borrowers are concerned that they will make the situation worse. However, statistics in 2008 showed that lenders typically lose about $50,000 on average on every foreclosure. They do not want to foreclose any more than you want them to. So the first step is to contact your lender and see what they can do for you. Options can include:

1. *Balance refinance.* Although you may not qualify in the general market, your lender will look at your circumstances and your ability to pay going forward and may be able to provide a balance refinance to cure the delinquency and give you a fresh start when others cannot.

2. *Loan modification or recast.* If you do not qualify for a re-finance, or the lender does not have that option available, the lender may be able to do a modification to the rate and terms of your current mortgage to extend the past due payments to the end, modify the interest rate to make the loan more affordable, and change the term.

3. *Repayment plan.* If you can afford the current payments but cannot make up the past due payments, your lender may be able to provide a modified repayment plan to catch up the past due payments over time.

4. *Reinstatement or forbearance.* Another potential option is a reinstatement or forbearance. This is where the lender temporarily agrees to delay payments for a short period of time if you can prove you'll eventually acquire funds to bring the past due payments current from sources such as a tax refund, gift, or bonus.

5. *Balance reduction.* Your lender may be willing to reduce your balance so you can finance with another lender and pay them off.

6. *Short sale.* Your lender may agree to a short sale, that is, let you sell your home for an amount less than you owe. In this situation, you want to get a short-sale price pre-approval letter to submit to your Realtor. This is a common practice used in situations where the property value has depreciated due to a severe drop in the real estate market. The key with both the short sale and balance reduction is to ask for the lender to agree to the terms without nega-tively affecting your credit. Many lenders will agree to this to avoid foreclosure and lessen their losses.

7. *Deed in lieu of foreclosure.* The last resort is what is called a deed in lieu of foreclosure. This is where you simply deed the property back to the lender. Unfortunately, in most cases this will result in harming your credit severely and may result in a repayment of the shortage over time. However, depending on the deal you negotiate with your lender, it can at least absolve you of the immediate debt and payments.

I would recommend you talk to your lender about all of these options to see which is best for your situation and involve legal counsel in the process.

Government and Lender Refinance Programs

There are many refinance programs for borrowers with poor credit or those in foreclosure. The Federal Housing Administration is a leader in this with programs like their FHA Secure Program that was developed in 2007. These programs can be accessed through any FHA approved lender. There are specific conditions that must exist for a borrower to qualify for these programs. These include things like: history of on-time mortgage payments, specific reasons for the delinquency, specific LTV requirements, sustained employment, and sufficient income. To get a list of the most recent programs, search on-line or visit FHA's Web site at www.myfha.net

Counseling

In any of these situations, my advice is to seek wise counsel. "The lips of the wise give good advice; the heart of a fool has none to give," the proverb says.[2] The key is finding a reputable, honest, and knowledgeable counselor who can help you with your financial situation. Your accountant or financial advisor is a good place to start.

Turn It Over to God

All of the suggestions I have given you hinge on human effort. However, as important as that is, difficulties like mortgage delinquency and foreclosure are devastating. The stress and pressure can be unbearable. When all of our human efforts have failed, it may be time to turn it over to a power way beyond ours—the power of God. If God can create the universe and something as beautiful and intricate as you, He can also provide calm in difficult times. I have learned this hundreds of times in my life. The Bible provides comfort here: "Do not be anxious about anything, but in everything, by prayer and petition, with thanksgiving, present your requests to God."[3]

I will talk more about the role of faith and our relationship with God in the next chapter. The Scriptures do assure us of comfort, of a God who promises rest for our souls in the midst of heavy burdens.[4]

NOTES

1. Ephesians 5:15–16.
2. Proverbs 15:7.
3. Philippians 4:6 (NIV).
4. See especially Matthew 11:28–30.

CHAPTER ELEVEN

MOVING TO REAL LIFE
Change

This book has been dedicated to providing education to help you achieve financial success in your mortgage, debt, and overall wealth. The goal of these financial facts, concepts, statistical data, and even analytical formulas has been to help you recapture wealth that was being wasted on interest and debt so it can be used for more significant purposes, like education, retirement, investments, and charitable giving. I am confident that, at this point, you are looking at a mortgage as much more than just a financial transaction, but as a major life event. Because financial success affects nearly every aspect of your life, I want to encourage you to apply the knowledge you have gained.

Money—The Road to True Happiness?

But as important as financial success is, it is just a small part of a much bigger story. The book of Psalms, a collection of poems and songs found in the Bible from historic leaders like Israel's King David, includes this advice:

◇◇◇

And if your wealth increases, don't make it the center of your life.
(Psalm 62:10)

◇◇◇

Although the strategies in this book may increase our wealth as it pertains to our mortgage and finances, we want to be careful not to make any newfound wealth the center of our lives. This is a very easy trap to fall into—one I fell into myself years ago. Let me begin this chapter by telling you part of my story.

I was born in the United States in a suburb outside of Chicago. My mom and dad were hardworking and loving parents who, for most of my childhood, struggled financially to put food on the table. Although we had a close-knit family, I did not get to see much of my parents, particularly my dad; both worked long hours to pay the bills. My dad was a construction worker and my mom cleaned houses, cooked, and worked at a local supermarket. During the winters, when my dad would be laid off from work, he would fish all day to put food on the table, then collect newspapers and copper wire to take to the junkyard so his kids could have a Christmas. My parents were good and honest people, and two of the hardest workers I have ever met. We were a typical lower-to-middle-class family.

In 1976, my life changed forever. During the spring, my dad was involved in a work accident that nearly took his life. He spent several weeks in intensive care and several months in the hospital. We spent many nights by his hospital bed, not sure if he would be alive the next day. Then, during the summer of that same year, my seventeen-year-old brother, Jesse, died in a drowning accident. I was there when the divers pulled his body out of the water and could do nothing to help. Our family's lives had been shattered.

For the next several years, I acted as the head of the household. My dad was on a long road to recovery from his accident and was in and out of the hospital for nearly two years. My mom and dad were unable to live out their normal roles as parents due to both physical limitations my dad faced and the emotional suffering caused by their broken hearts. At the young age of fourteen, I became an adult. I was scared, confused, and mad at God.

Those three years after Jesse's death, before I went off into the working world, changed me in many ways. It led to a volatile temper, excessive drinking, and an unhealthy desire to succeed. Maybe this desire for success came from the years of struggle and a longing to get *more* out of life. Maybe it was from the three years I was lost in the shadows from the grief of my parents. Maybe it was a response to the loss of my brother and the personal sorrow that accompanied that. Maybe it was just a need for acceptance. Whatever it was, like so many, I worked long hours and missed out on so much of life, all in pursuit of the next pay increase, the next job title, and the next achievement.

Achievement and Wealth—Let's Go!

Fast-forward to age thirty. I had recently married my wife, Laurel, my best friend, the love of my life, and the most amazing woman I have ever known. We had a two-year-old son, an infant, and another baby due "soon." I was still seeking achievement, success, and wealth. And after ten years in the mortgage industry, I had worked my way up from a loan officer with no college degree to a senior executive of a national mortgage company with responsibility for over a thousand employees. I was making a six-figure income, owned a beautiful new house, and had just bought my dream car. I had finally made it financially. Happiness was surely going to be mine now!

One day in 1996, I was sitting at my desk and realized that my work and wealth *did not* bring me the happiness that I had hoped for. The recognition, promotions, and pay raises were never enough. The career I dreamed of and worked so hard for required me to work long hours and be away from the family I dearly loved. I realized the money and lifestyle I thought I always wanted was not as fulfilling once I had achieved it. I finally understood the saying "The joy is in the journey, not the destination."

I had achieved what I thought was the mountaintop financially and yet had a semitruck-size void in my heart. I had learned, firsthand, an important truth:

◇◇◇

**Wealth and possessions are not the highway
to happiness or fulfillment.**

◇◇◇

My story may sound familiar to you. Maybe you have experienced the same thing. Or maybe you are thinking, *I have never known what it is like to have financial wealth or success. I have struggled my whole life just to make ends meet.* Having lived over two-thirds of my life the same way, I understand your feelings. Although you may not have achieved the kind of financial wealth I am referring to and may not feel "wealthy," the fact that you own (or are thinking of buying) a home puts you in the top 5 percent in wealth worldwide.

I can tell you from experience that even if you had financial wealth beyond your dreams, it would not be the root of your happiness.

◇◇◇

**True wealth has little to do with money.
It is wealth in a much fuller sense that goes
well beyond money.**

◇◇◇

Financial wealth and success is fragile at best. If I ended this book by just focusing on financial wealth and success, it would fall short of providing the life-changing knowledge I want you to have in the critical areas of life that really matter—your family, your legacy, and your faith!

Let's take a deeper look at the true role that money, wealth, and possessions should play in our lives from a biblical perspective. We will look at how to build a personal and financial legacy and true life success. In doing so, I will offer several nuggets of wisdom and encouragement that have made a profound difference in my life, and I hope will in yours, too!

Money Is *Not* Central to Our Lives!

Much of this book has talked about money. I hope that has not led to the perception that money is central to our lives. Money is *integral* to our lives, but certainly not *central*. Nearly all of us have been fooled into thinking that having more money will lead to more happiness. After all, money allows us to do things that bring enjoyment.

Think about this for a minute: How many people can you think of who have achieved financial success and "security," but have lived heartbreaking and shattered lives? I could fill the pages of this book with their names. In his book *Success*, Glenn Bland describes nine of the wealthiest men in the world and what happened at the end of their lives: Four went broke, three committed suicide, one died insane, and one went to prison.

If you look at the lives of people recently in the news, you will come up with a dozen examples instantly. People in the entertainment industry, professional athletes, politicians, CEOs ... the list goes on and on. All of these people experienced an age-old truth from their fame and fortune: *Money does not, cannot, and will not bring you complete happiness, security, or fulfillment.* Here's what the Bible has to say about wealth and its pursuit: "But people who long to be rich fall into temptation and are trapped by many foolish and harmful desires that plunge them into ruin and destruction."[1]

We could apply all of the financial strategies, techniques, and wisdom presented in this book to create the best financial stability for ourselves and our family, and still one major life event could change all of that in a moment! A loss of employment, major health issue, change in the economy, natural disaster, or other catastrophic event, and everything we have worked so hard for could disappear.

Clearly, we live in an uncertain world during uncertain times. Ultimately, there is no guaranteed stability in the economy, or in our wealth or possessions. As the Scripture clearly teaches, "Those who are rich in this world [are] not to be proud and not to trust in their money, which is so unreliable" (1 Timothy 6:17).

A Centuries-Old Perspective on True Wealth and Happiness

The truth that our happiness and fulfillment will never come from our wealth—our money or possessions—is not new. About 900 BC King Solomon, himself the richest king in the richest kingdom of that time, wrote:

◇◇◇

"Those who love money will never have enough. How meaningless to think that wealth brings true happiness!" (Ecclesiastes 5:10)

◇◇◇

King Solomon had it figured out thousands of years ago. When it came to power, prestige, possessions, and wealth, you would have to go a long way in history to find anyone who had more. He became the king of Israel in 970 BC and had riches and wealth beyond anything we can ever imagine.[2] Financially speaking, he was the Bill Gates of his generation.

Yet with all of his fame and fortune, near the end of his life Solomon wrote the book of Ecclesiastes to define true happiness and address issues like work, wealth, and possessions. Here is more of what he had to say:

> There is another serious problem I have seen under the sun. Hoarding *riches* harms the saver. *Money is put into risky investments that turn sour, and everything is lost.* In the end, there is nothing left to pass on to one's children. We all come to the end of our lives naked and empty-handed as on the day we were born. *We can't take our riches with us.*
>
> And this, too, is a very serious problem. *People leave this world no better off than when they came.* All their hard work is for nothing—like working for the wind. Throughout their lives, they live under a cloud—frustrated, discouraged, and angry. (Ecclesiastes 5:13–17, italics added)

Without reading further, one would surmise that Solomon needed a cappuccino and a motivational video! He comes across as a bitter, depressed, and negative old king. Nothing could be further from the truth. King Solomon was not only the richest man of his day, and possibly in history, but has been referred to as the wisest man who ever lived.[3] He wrote most of the Proverbs, which are among the most famous and quoted sayings in history. This same Solomon continues on in verses 18 to 19. Note what he says next:

> Even so, I have noticed one thing, at least, that is good. It is good for people to *eat, drink, and enjoy their work* under the sun during the short life God has given them, and to *accept their lot in life*. And it is a good thing to *receive wealth from God and the good health to enjoy it*. To enjoy your work and accept your lot in life—this is indeed a gift from God. (italics added)

As you can see, in Solomon's long, prosperous, and successful life, he learned some valuable lessons. He learned that *life is not all about working for riches*. Notice that Solomon referred to the acquiring of money as "riches," not "wealth," (in verses 13–17) and called it a "serious problem" (unhappiness). Then he contrasted this by referring to wealth as "one thing, at least, that is good" (happiness, perhaps?). But Solomon did not use these two words, *riches* and *wealth*, interchangeably, as we do today. He used them as two distinctively different words with two different meanings. In this writing, Solomon redefines wealth as something far different from riches. Let's expand this thought.

Look at the first segment again. When talking about the serious problems he saw in life, he referred to the harm that comes from "hoarding riches." He states the truth, *"We can't take our riches with us."* There is another old saying I have always liked that goes like this: "You will never see a hearse pulling a U-haul!" Moral of the story: We cannot take money with us when we are gone, so we might as well make the most of it while we are here.

King Solomon relates wealth to people, celebration (eat and drink), work, and health. Solomon focuses on the things that really matter. He defines what brings us true happiness and joy: being with people we love, sharing meals we like, accepting our work with joy, and having good health. He uses the word *wealth* in the context of the *totality* of these things, not in having lots of money (as we tend to see the word used today). Solomon saw riches as a serious problem, but wealth as good. He also used words like *enjoy* and *accept*.

Wise King Solomon teaches us that wealth is much more than money; it is living a life accepting who we are and enjoying the people and calling in our life.

True Wealth Is a Gift

Solomon also provides one more profound insight about true wealth: It is indeed a gift from God! Solomon recognized that *he* does not provide all the good things (the people, or the food, or the drink, or even the work)—it is all a gift from God. The beauty of viewing all good things as gifts is that it creates an appreciation for the Giver!

◇◇◇

When we view everything in life as a gift from God, it makes us want to respond with thankfulness and reciprocation.

◇◇◇

So what is *one way* we can reciprocate the gifts we have been given by God? By giving back to others!

Here's another saying you have heard many times: "It is more blessed to give than to receive."[4] Did you know that Jesus of Nazareth said those words? Giving to others is one of the many ways we achieve true wealth. It is also the primary way we build our legacy.

Building a Legacy by Giving Back

What will be your legacy? Perhaps you have pondered the question, "What will people say and think about me well after I am gone?" It's a critical question to ask. Each of us will die one day. As the old saying goes, "Death is as unavoidable as paying taxes." Although we do not know when or how that will happen, we know *it will happen*—there is no avoiding it. That means that we are building our legacy today! So what is the most important factor that will determine our legacy? It is what, how, and to whom we give back in our lifetimes. The three primary legacies we leave behind are:

1. *Our personal legacy.* How will we be remembered; what will be our lasting impact? Our personal legacy will span four areas: (1) *our integrity*, or what we stood for during our lives; (2) *our impact*, i.e., how we poured our lives into others; (3) *our involvement*, i.e., how we participated in our community and the world at large; and (4) *our inheritance*: how we led our families and the impact their lives will have on others.

2. *Our financial legacy.* What we do with the wealth (money and possessions) we have accumulated (no matter the amount).
3. *Our belief legacy.* The traditions, beliefs, and moral code we hand down to future generations.

I'm sure you will agree that these legacies are far greater than having riches. Here are ways to create your personal, financial, and belief legacies.

Building Our Personal Legacy

In our quest to build a legacy of *integrity*, let's remember that this is the one character trait that all of us control. Our integrity during our lives will ultimately dictate how we are remembered. My favorite definition of integrity is from Dr. Ron Jenson, a dear friend and author of the book *Achieving Authentic Success*:

◇◇◇

"Personality is what we are in public, character is what we are in private, and integrity is when they are the same!"

◇◇◇

Are you the same in public as in private? What do you stand for? Do you stand for what is good and right? Will you be remembered as a person of honesty and integrity? These are character traits that endure over time. Ask yourself the question, "If I died today, how will I be remembered years after I am gone?" By living our lives today in a way that stands for integrity, we will be remembered for many generations and will have a profound impact on the integrity of our descendants.

To build a legacy of impact, we must pour our lives into

others. The focus here is not quantity, but quality. By making a significant difference in just one person's life, you have made an *impact*. Think what this world would look like if everyone lived by that simple objective—we would change an entire culture!

In the movie *Pay It Forward*, based on the bestselling novel by Catherine Ryan Hyde, fifth grade teacher Eugene Simonet (played by Kevin Spacey) challenges his class to come up with an idea that can "change the world." One student, Trevor McKinney (Haley Joel Osment), comes up with a profoundly simple solution: If everyone did something nice for three other people, who "paid it forward" by doing something nice for three more people, eventually everyone's life would be changed in some small but positive way.

You might be thinking, as I did, *How many times would you have to pay it forward to change the lives of 7.5 billion people worldwide?* Amazingly, the answer is *only* eighteen times! As you can see, we can make a significant impact by simply helping others one person at a time! What impact are you having on others?

Our *involvement* in our community and the world at large is another important part of our personal legacy. What we do in and for our community can have both a local and global impact that can last for decades. Whether we are spending time working at a soup kitchen, helping at a shelter for people who are abused, or involved in a charity event, our involvement can change the lives of the people we come in contact with. Because of the global community we now live in, we never know how far reaching the impact of our involvement in things can be.

Not only do you change the lives of the people you are involved with in some way, but your actions also set a standard for others to follow. Here is another saying from the book of Proverbs: "Do not withhold good from those who deserve it when it is in your power to help them" (3:27). What are you involved in that will leave a mark on this world?

To build your legacy of *inheritance*, focus on giving and influencing your family. How we lead our families, the way we raise our children, and the way we treat our spouse will affect their lives and the lives of others. As parents, we can never forget or minimize the impact we have on our kids. This is something I am still trying to learn daily as a dad. We are products of our parents, good or bad, and so are our children. What we do, more than what we say, molds our children into who they are. Our children carry on our family name and behaviors. They are a direct legacy of our leadership. The way we treat our spouse also has a profound impact on our children and our marriage. This also is true for our extended family—parents, siblings, and relatives.

Take time with those you love. Do not be too busy trying to "make a living" that you forget about the ones who really matter in your life. We are not getting any younger, nor are they. Remember, on our deathbed none of us will long for another day at work! We will long for more time with those we love. We have that time today, so make the most of it. Once you lose time, you can never get it back!

Building Our Financial Legacy

Our financial legacy comes from what we do with the money and possessions we have accumulated (no matter the amount) and what we give back to others. This means both (1) being wise with our money so as to teach others how to manage the money that is given to them and (2) sharing our money with those who are less fortunate. For some of us, because we are struggling just to make ends meet, giving some of the little we have seems unrealistic. Our financial legacy is not determined by the amount of money we give, but by how generous we are with it. In other words, *our use of and generosity with money determines our true financial legacy.* This comes from our *attitude* toward money. Here is a great example of this from the Bible:

> Jesus sat down opposite the place where the offerings were put and watched the crowd putting their money into the temple treasury. Many rich people threw in large amounts. But a poor widow came and put in two very small copper coins, worth only a fraction of a penny. Calling his disciples to him, Jesus said, "I tell you the truth, this poor widow has put more into the treasury than all the others. They all gave out of their wealth; but she, out of her poverty, put in everything—all she had to live on."[5]

Jesus' teaching here is simple: It is not important how much we give, but that we give from the heart. That is what ultimately matters. What is not important is how much we give, but whether we *are* giving and our attitude about giving. Generosity is an act of love. Think of it this way: If everyone gave *something,* how much of the world's poverty, illiteracy, and hunger would be solved?

My sons and I have had the incredible opportunity to travel to rural India several times and meet thousands of children and their families in both the orphanages we support and the villages we serve. This has been a life-changing experience for all of us. People are literally dying in the streets from malnutrition. After visiting India the first time, not only did I realize how much we as Americans have, but what a difference even a few dollars can make. When you consider that the average Indian worker makes about five dollars a week, it quickly becomes apparent that any kind of giving makes a profound difference. Although we cannot stop starvation or help as many as we would like, we can begin to make a difference one life at a time.

There are many who are poor and suffering in our own communities. What a difference we can make when we contribute to charities and needy people both in the United States and abroad. Remember, "Whoever sows generously will also reap generously."[6]

The satisfaction and joy we receive in helping another human being in need yields a return one thousand times the investment! Make giving a cornerstone of your legacy today. Start giving back so you can leave something of greater value behind when you are gone—the changing of a human's life!

Building Our Belief Legacy

Let me end by asking you the two most important and life-affecting questions of this entire book:

> *What is the foundation of your core beliefs?*
> *What—or who—is in the "center" of your life?*

Our beliefs form the most important legacy we leave behind. They shape everything we do, everything we are, and everything we stand for. Our beliefs are the foundation for both the moral code and traditions we pass down to our future generations. What we believe forms our faith and is central to our life and legacy. Our faith interacts with and impacts every aspect of our lives. So let me ask you this equally important question: "What is your faith in?"

Several years ago I met a man in his thirties who tried to honestly answer this question. At the end of one of my training seminars, I posed that question to the audience. Afterward, this man, who I'll call Eric, approached me with his answer. After long reflection, he came to the realization that he had faith in *nothing!*

I immediately asked Eric four questions: (1) How did he come to the event?, (2) why did he stay all day?, (3) what will he do with what he had learned?, and (4) what do you plan to do with the success you may achieve? His responses were that he had driven his car to the event; he stayed all day because he had learned a lot; he intended to apply the new skills he had learned to his life; and he planned to use his newfound success to achieve the happiness he had always dreamed of.

From his answers we determined four very important things: (1) he had *faith* that his car would get him to the event safely; (2) he had *faith* that the things I had taught him would help him succeed; (3) he had *faith* in his ability to achieve success; and (4) he had *faith* that his success and financial gain would lead to happiness. I ended our conversation by saying, "Eric, a minute ago you told me you had faith in nothing. But if I heard you right, you have now told me you have faith in at least four things: *your car, me, yourself,* and *money.* The problem is that all of these things are temporary. Cars rust, people let us down, we all make mistakes, and money never brings happiness. The real question I would ask you to consider is what your *core faith* is *really in*."

In the end Eric admitted that his eyes had been opened to some new thoughts and agreed that it was time to do a little soul searching.

The moral of the story: *We all have faith in something.*

We all have faith in something or someone. The critical question is *What or who is in the center?* Whatever is at the center of our lives represents our foundational beliefs and, therefore, becomes our "god" (note the small "g," not big "G").

The Search for the Perfect God

Recall at one point I was making a six-figure income, owned a beautiful new house, and had just bought my dream car. At age thirty, I had surpassed every goal I had set out to attain. I had acquired the things I thought I always wanted: a wonderful family, a high position, the respect of my peers, financial wealth, and possessions. But, in spite of all of this, I still felt that hole in my heart. So one day I sat down and drew a series of concentric circles on a piece of paper, starting with a center circle and bigger circles around it. In each of the outer circles I filled in the things in my life I had acquired that mattered to me. I left the center circle blank.

You see, I was trying to determine what was at the *center* of my life. I was trying to figure out what or who made all of the other circles work. It was at that very moment that it hit me—I had put myself in the center. My god was an imperfect me! I instantly determined that I *did not* want to and *could not* be in the center. I did not want that much pressure and responsibility. I also knew, somewhere deep in my soul, that I did not have the wisdom, power, ability, or authority to control all of those "circles" in my life. That day I realized that the hole in my heart was nothing more than a longing for *true happiness* that could be filled only by a perfect God (big "G").

I had what I refer to as "my Solomon moment" that day. I realized that I was looking for true happiness in things that were temporary, not eternal. I was trying to control my universe and had no power to do so. I had come to a low enough point in my life to realize that what I was really longing for was someone who had *the ability to love me unconditionally, the power to forgive me for all of the wrongs I had committed and give me a new start, and the wisdom to guide every aspect of my life.* I knew the God the Bible spoke of was the only possible candidate who could provide this.

Up to that point in my life, I had not believed that this kind of God really existed, and I doubted much of what the Bible taught. Now I was willing to at least do some searching.

I had turned away from God and blamed Him for the bad things that had happened in my life. Experientially, I had seen so many examples of hypocrisy in the church and from "religious" people that the whole idea of religion turned me off. Intellectually, I could not accept the things I had heard and read in the Bible because I could not prove them and had not seen them for myself. Emotionally, I could not understand how a "loving God" could take my brother, devastate our family, and let me wander into all kinds of troubles that led to pain, suffering, and guilt. Yet I still knew that I needed to learn about God, find out who Jesus really was, and test what the Bible claimed to be Truth. That day, my personal journey of faith began.

Ironically, at the same time my wife was also having the same kind of questions in her life. Only her questions came from our thirteen-year-old babysitter, who had asked her about her beliefs about Jesus. For the next three months, together with my wife and her encouragement, I attended a local church she had been going to and met weekly with one of the pastors. Every Sunday I challenged him, throwing his way every reason I thought the Bible was not true, God was not loving, and Jesus could not be the Son of God. He had a logical and biblical answer for every question and sound reasoning for those things that still are simply based on faith. What really had the biggest impact, however, were not his answers to my questions or caring concern for me, but the change I saw in my wife's life and the love I saw in the people I met in the church.

◇◇◇

Lasting change from the inside out cannot be achieved through human effort.

◇◇◇

At age thirty-one, I made a leap of faith and committed my life to Jesus Christ. For the first time, the hole in my heart was filled. I felt a peace I had never known before. *Nothing* has been the same since.

In the fifteen years since that decision, my life has changed in countless ways. My temper, my excessive drinking, and my endless pursuit of success, wealth, and possessions have all gone away. I could write an entire book just on the changes I have experienced in my life and the lives of thousands of others I have met in my travels across the world. But let me just sum it up by saying that all the changes in my life did not happen naturally, but supernaturally. For years I tried, through books, seminars, and tapes, to change myself from the outside in and only saw temporary change in my life. Since making Jesus the center of my life, I have seen lasting change from the inside out that cannot be achieved through human effort or explained by human intellect. I finally found the "love that surpasses knowledge."

You may be able to relate to key elements of my personal story. All of us have suffered pain and loss in our life. All of us have felt lonely and unloved. Jesus said, "Come to me, all of you who are weary and carry heavy burdens, and I will give you rest."[7] He also made a bold declaration that He can meet our personal needs and understands our suffering and loss. After all, history tells us that He traveled the areas in and around Jerusalem for over three years with little more than the clothes on His back to help the poor, heal the sick, and preach a message of peace, only to be arrested, beaten, and later suffer a brutal death on the cross.

He told His followers two millennia ago, "Here on earth you will have many trials and sorrows. But take heart, because I have overcome the world."[8]

Beyond our pain and loss, we may feel regret from our mistakes and even remorse and guilt from those choices. As the Bible says, "All have sinned and fall short of the glory of God."[9] Jesus says He has come from God to offer us forgiveness, true happiness, and freedom from pain and suffering.

All of these things are available to us for *free* through God— *It is the deal of the century!*

What Does It Mean to Follow Jesus?

Let me clarify something important: Following Jesus is not about *religion*, but about *relationship*. Nowhere in the Bible does it say, "If you do these things, *then* I will love and accept you." Instead, it tells us that Jesus loves and accepts us as we are. All Jesus asks us to do is believe in Him and who He said He is—the Son of God who died for our sins. Following Jesus is not about following rules, but loving Him. Following Jesus is not about performance—we do not have to achieve anything for Him to love and accept us. Finally, following Jesus is not about being perfect, because once we give our life to Him, He sees us as being perfect even while we are not. After all, we are made in His image!

When we make Jesus the center of our lives and trust in Him, we no longer need to carry the burdens and pressure of trying to control every aspect of our circumstances, but instead can trust that He has our back covered and our best interest in mind.

Let me close with a simple summary of what the Bible offers you and me, and a few Bible verses to support this.

First, the Bible tells us that Jesus died for our imperfections and mistakes (our sins) so that we may be forgiven and can be reunited with God, who is perfect. "God's *free gift* leads to our being made right with God, even though we are guilty of many sins."[10]

God is holy, and it matters not how minor the sin or good our intentions. Our bad choices affect not only us personally but also everyone around us. Consider this: If you have a perfectly white piece of paper and then put the smallest black smudge on it, is it still perfectly white? Of course not. The same holds true for our relationship with God. God is the perfect white paper and our sin is the smudge. We cannot be in His presence unless we, too, are perfectly white. Knowing that none of us is perfect, we can only be made that way through the forgiveness of our sin and through the cleansing of the "smudge." This was done through Jesus, the perfect God-man, coming to earth, living a prefect life and then dying on the cross to accept our punishment for our sin. He is the perfect sacrifice.

Second, we must believe that Jesus is God's Son and place Him in the center of our lives. In one of the most famous verses in the Bible, Jesus declared that He is the Son of God and that eternal life comes to those who believe in Him: "For God so loved the world that he gave his one and only Son, that whoever believes in him shall not perish but have eternal life."[11]

"Believe in him" means to trust Him with our lives, to put Him in the center. When we accept Him as Savior from our sins, we are wiped clean of all sins. And, Jesus says, we will spend eternity with God in heaven, an eternity without pain and suffering.[12]

This decision not only affects us eternally, but it affects us in the here and now. When we believe in Jesus as the Son of God, our life will be made "new." The Scriptures put it this way: "This means that anyone who belongs to Christ has become a *new person*. The old life is gone; a *new life* has begun! . . . Put on your *new nature*, and be renewed as you learn to know your Creator and become like him."[13]

As I mentioned earlier, so many things have changed in my life since I made the decision to follow Jesus. These were things I had no personal power to change. He changed them in me. This is the biggest reason I believe Jesus is who He says He is. I have experienced a dramatic change in my life from the inside out that cannot be explained in human terms. I have met thousands who have done and seen the same. People who have been saved from all kinds of addictions, were healed of illnesses, had reparation to relationships, and felt the burden of stress and depression lifted from their lives. I've met many who experienced freedom in days from what they couldn't break for years!

All of this is ours with one simple decision—a decision to acknowledge our faults, to ask God to be the center of our life, and to trust and follow Him. *All it takes is faith!*

If you, like I, have experienced pain and suffering in your life and long for true happiness, I would encourage you to make this decision of faith today.

Where Do I Go from Here?

If you want to learn more about the life of faith in Jesus Christ, I would first encourage you to pick up a New International Version or New Living Translation version of the Bible and see what it has to say. I would recommend reading the books of John, James, Colossians, and Romans for starters. I believe you will find the answers you have been searching for.

If you want recommendations on additional resources to help you in this journey, please visit our Web site at www.mortgagempowered.com. I invite you to get one of our free *Winning in the Game of Life* DVDs, where I share my story and answers to questions of faith in greater detail.

NOTES

1. 1 Timothy 6:9.
2. 1 Kings 10:14–25.
3. See 1 Kings 10:4–7.
4. Acts 20:35.

5. Mark 12:41–44 (NIV).

6. 2 Corinthians 9:6 (NIV).

7. Matthew 11:28.

8. John 16:33.

9. Romans 3:23 (NIV).

10. Romans 5:16 (italics added).

11. John 3:16 (NIV).

12. See John 14:1–3; Revelation 21:4.

13. 2 Corinthians 5:17; Colossians 3:10 (italics added).

THE SHORTEST
INVESTMENT BOOK EVER

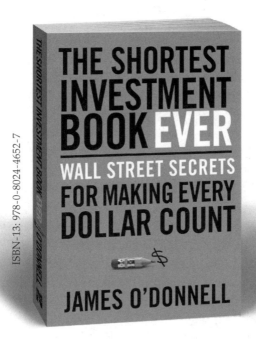

This book gives the facts—just the facts—on saving and investing for retirement in words everyone can understand. A former Wall Street pro, James O'Donnell uses simple, concise terms in a readable style to address the most crucial issues that affect your future financial health—whether you know it now or not!

MOODY
PUBLISHERS.

1-800-678-8812 · MOODYPUBLISHERS.COM